UNCONSCIOUS ACTS OF CANNIBALISM

UNCONSCIOUS ACTS OF CANNIBALISM

Spin Forever Downward

A COLLECTION OF WORKS BY

Edward Perkovich

To order additional copies of this book, contact:
Xlibris Corporation
1-888-795-4274
www.Xlibris.com
Orders@Xlibris.com
21229

"Ideas flicker uncontested, so close to the surface that
their denial could only be intentional, even if their unutilized
acceptance seems as pointless as finishing this sentence.
It's far too easy to be sober and grave."

—(Jimmy Keeper)

(Once lost) random, cocaine smokin' dithyramb
or
Goodmornin'

Welcome to the last thought you had before sleep filled your veins (with today's remains) and all that's known can be spoken in a single breath. Pretend for a moment, or for the rest of our lives that now, it would at least be something if you could turn your demon filled days into some form of tangible, emotional milkshake; uncorking the Gin Bottle Blues, releasing your self-absorbed stomach ache upon the half-blind, the tone deaf, the callous passers' of time and attention, knowing fever dreams to be at least 49% real one odd colored Hunger Artist has only to blink to resume breathing.

Ignition, injection, uncontradiction's restriction. The spontaneous choice to do a whole lot of nothin'. Makin' sense of dollars and silent hollers; the crowd gathers alone, speaks written words, stands a sit-down strike, protests the arrest of freedoms leaders [(shaded by cedars cut-down for grazin', brought to attention.) thinking of redemption, every single group awakens at noon to see what was heard] hearing this, "This incantation, one past two, oui monsieur, a three time loser, sentenced to isolation (a bleeder and boozier)."

First, speak your last/one word will suffice, so with balls in hand and curtain closing soon, the roar wasn't heard as your eyes spoke 'noon.' Second, speaking again//as far as last words go, you could have gave it some thought, one would think!?! So you do dream, dream big dreams and to you I think I'll drink. And cheers were given.

UNWANTED

With unity at the heart of Nature
    chaos adorns the extremities, masking the moment in which
darkness mocks dream and everything combusts upon impact
                        with lastweek's lust, leaving
ashen shadows
where once stood simple songs, blendind imagery and language with
                         booze and blisters,
knowing now too well

      the screams of the hollow awaken dark, hidden fears
                    with no way to the surface light
cannot escape from this wide-open plane,
         facing the sun/setting even with the valley//fading softly
(right on time) into tomorrow wherein those moments, blurry at best, fall
like autumn and everything learned combusts upon re-entry;
         combining ash and atmosphere, breathed-in by the masses,
reabsorbed by the blood stream/streaming back to the front of Natures
ironic iron-lung,
                  and all that was
unwanted
unites with what was best
        and what did actually happen.

... BOOZE, BREAD, BEANS, ...
OR
I FEEL BETTER IN THE
FETAL POSITION

After 3 genuine attempts to set the parking-lot on fire I'd given-up and started to walkincircles. Completing a satisfactory number of laps around my half-paid-for '85 GMC Jimmy, I then proceeded to sprint back to the belltower, making sure (for the fourth time) that my scope was unfogged, my vodka martini was dry and every registered voter wore a cowbell around their neck, so I wouldn't have to take my eyes off the prize, cuz ya know how much I can't stand conversations that begin; i mean, in reference to, because of the ending (that is nonexistent) knows nothing but,

1. the NOW
2. Currier and Ives
3. unnecessarily obscure references
4. a small print shopping list that reads as follows: laundry(get or due), check(signover), candles, incense, showersoap, dishsoap, mouthsoap, booze, bread, beans, vials of Anthrax(4), 14 year-old virgin(??), 7oz. sheep plasma, cooking oil, peanut oil, motor oil, oil of olay, soil(3yds.), leftover leftovers, new socks, old socks(see laundry), 1/2 oz. marijuana, plant food, a plant or two, fresh air, air in the tires, spare tire, tire jack, jack-in-the-box, a box, something to put in the box, . . . and on and on it went. I found the list while walking towards my group evaluation. I arrived to find an empty room, save a single parchment addressed to me. And their list reads as follows: Noticeable Imperfections; hell is where all screams come from and from heaven flow all tears, so there's been a rediscovery of the origins

of earthquakes and rain, now what you say?!? "now what indeed," is whispered in my good ear[(without it occurring to me how sensual a whisper can be). Think about it, no, try it, go up to an acquaintance/friend/lover/classmate and whisper this harmless phrase, "how about you and I go for a walk,"]. One could be setting up a drug-deal, getting "some air", making a physical threat, making surprise party plans, . . . but in a dark bedroom or a pew in church; the soft/warm/secretive/moist/velvet whisper of a breeze and a breath, a breath dissolving context clues, allowing one to act and in this scenario the action is to go for a walk. Now what indeed?!? Go to the bar, go to the bathroom and vomit these thoughts, that booze, this lunch, a waist of time, it was all a waist of time. Walkingincircles as I walkincircles for a minute or two or until I don't know what I want to do, then I go and do it.

It's one of those things where once it is spoken, it'll be taken wrong.

EUCLIDEAN ALGORITHM

savage acceptance of time's drooling shadow increases deception,
ringing an echoed number chase to the N*th* degree of an acoustic
backlash with
dreamtimes's sublime fine wine. self-aware salvation + absolute
substitution = a
reversing of sdrawkcab thinking into truth's irreverent denial
(for not preparing) accelerates a disproportionate whitewashed window /
whereupon the music of the spheres,
bleeding velvet headgear
and now known nonsense articulates broken speech,
broken word, broken verse
and
all patient patients slowly soothe
sight,
songs
and
such.

DA TAGTE ES

redeem the surrogate goodbyes
the sheet astreem in your hand
who have no more for the land
and the glass unmisted above your eyes

—SAMUEL BECKETT

MARRY the VINE to the ELM

Tell me of that which you know, that which flows throughout arteries and veins, but flows not from the lips. The lips that accept truth's noble challenge, blowing away (into undetectable particles) yesterday and all that it was, while kissing (ever so softly) what may or may not be right. Tell me of that which you know, what appears to be sound but, falls not from the mouth, what makes you whole and yet burns you hollow (inside-out). Tell me that you believe in the resilient human emotional arsenal, that you can inflate your underdeveloped pride and that you cryout to hear your breath echo against peace or treason, or whatever water into which you wade. Tell me of that which you know only if the ease of yours will allow and my similar song I'll sing, so all that lets us breathe will know thine illusions that accompany us to rest and together we shall know one another (best than separate, alone, each we fall).

It was not all that long of a while before the pleasure recoiled, absorbed by the overworked parts of metabolism's better interest. It was not all that long ago / in terms of motion past // in terms of what was; that *he* sat on the shore, boarding sea and land, that he sat on

13

shore, pickling and pealing and dying and thinking of the very last image he had conjured (seconds before sleep comfortably settled in atop the events of last week, lastnight, whenever). Sitting on the shore, rocking backandforth, quadriceps tight against the chest, hunger spiraling his will down into the sand, becoming an unoriginal emotional sacrifice, a silhouette of who he remembers being; all the while, covered in gold, out in the cold, internally bleeding and breathing and clinching and wondering why the previous 60 seconds of his life were spent (without interest) contemplating (without guilt) the minute prior to that. He would like to think that reasons were as tangible as the sails of his shipwrecked shipwreck. He would like to believe; life was his, everything became real once experienced and that the wind which covers tracks in sand, originates from previous times he (we) fell into sleep's all encompassing goo. He would like to take a short nap so that he would be awake to watch the sunset.

The last of his life drained from the openings in his body just as *she* happened across the beach.

She would like to think that in actuality, she's what compassion ate, why time would wait and that she could see his raw emotion helplessly drizzle onto beachglass, causing a sparkle gleam shimmer shine considered rare to living eyes. She did nothing unless she was told, said nothing unless she was asked and screamed outside for fear of being understood, thus becoming human and obtainable.

"You'd have ta be the loveliest creature in ALL of creation," she was often told. By many. Women and men alike. Domesticide she thought. She did not feel as if she was a creature, nor did she feel lovely. She wasn't even sure what lovely meant when the word was used in an expression that was applied to her; pleasing to the eye, a glowing physical beauty, something inside, in their demeanor, on the outside, shallow / lustful, kind of // a kind of kindness that revealed itself to others, but not one's ownself?? She did not feel lovely. She felt as does a zombie, knowing that earth's salt couldn't remind her of a world, inwhich, return to was a nonfactor. One more thing to ignore . . . . THINGS . . . . things is the word. Things that she didn't care to deal with, things he could not deal with, things—the things that occurred with or without them. THEM. That would be the word [(or a form of, indicating an inclusion of absolutely everything they have knowledge of) with the exception being this scenario imparticular.]

A frameless picture *I* painted last winter while the average person was up to their average waist in average snowfall, average cold and more snow. I have a modest house on the beach, it's where I cower when the eggshell world becomes "all too much." I am considered a success in the realworld, although I do not feel as if I could consider myself to be; lucky or quick, savage or penny-wise, a social success / a personal failure. I feel as if, I feel like a spider. A spider that builds its web, knowing that (most likely) by sun's rise the web will be but threads, dangling with gravity's nonconcern, and nothing more. Construction of my life continues on, appearing effortless, even while miles away from the happenings of this day. This day upon sleep's subtle break, you awaken tired, *I* awaken comfortable, *she* wakes saddened and *he* wakes hungry. HUNGRY. I've never gone hungry, I know not how the physical or mental ramifications would effect me; but, while I was back at home, a tired, hungry, depressed youngman forcibly entered my beach-house in search of selfadministered, humane treatment. Finding not comfort nor sustenance / salvation curdled, pure, uncut depression wrapped its Woodbine Vines around the last of his pride (and in a place that I did hide, my stash he did find). Ego was suppressed, handfuls he did ingest, my, oh my, what a way to go.

Now . . . .

. . . . when one loses love, one tends to cross a slim track of thought that briefly passes the "Perhaps that really wasn't love," station. That very same thought, callous in its attempt to justify, occurred to her after her first marriage ended. But not the second, oh no, that was a mistake, he was an asshole, a fucking asshole, a real / really bad mistake she knew she had made with that one. And now that her third, holy and legal unification between man and woman has just crumbled into the sea, it was time to re-evaluate, re-go over, or, well shit, just something!?! She decided to airout, to take a walk, a walk along the beach. Her first husband is a corporate lawyer who spends a good deal of the year in southeast Asia. Apparently they were still close enough that she had a key to his second vacation home, which is 2 miles down the beach from my one and only vacation home.

She let him die, he begged her to let him die and she complied. A drug overdose aggravated by malnutrition, hunger strains, exposure . . . . His heart exploded, or somethinglikethat. She sat next to his lifeless body and watched the sunset that he wanted to be awake to see. She enjoyed it for both of them, unaware that the sunset is what compelled his slowly rotting carcass to not drop dead in my upstairs, windowless bathroom. By moonlight she walked home and proceeded to get high on cocaine, dry gin and some colorful pills that were selected with care. The tide wrapped him up in nature's apathetic blanket, then carried his vacant flesh casing some distance off-shore. He washed up, like a lump of wet blankets, about 100 yards from her first husband's second vacation home, where a stranger found him the following sunrise. She attended his silent burial three days after telling the police that she had, "No idea whatsoever, who he was, or where he came from," and that was that. I had my contractor repair my door and install an alarm system adequate enough to suit the insurance company's needs.

Only minutes after my return to the beach, upon finding out exactly what was missing and knowing what had happened, I formulated the scenario (and played it out as a short story) while I walked through the rooms of my guilt. I met her days latter sitting on the beach outside my vacation home, watching the sunset. I sat next to her without an exchange of words / spoken a word, or words of it. IT. That's the word. IT never happened until IT was experienced. Together we reviled what we knew about IT, but only months after we were married (my first wife).

She refuses to return to that beach, but it is known, for the sun always sets with or without us.

SOAKING BACKSTAGE IN A POOL OF CARELESS DISCONTENT

timeless time line

treading on land mines

fills blank space

with the race

to hurry

and not worry

EDITORS NOTE: The author was tripping on mushrooms at a friends restaurant before writing this.

CAESER SALAD

i whisper to my salad

a poem known as a ballad

but in my face

a dry disgrace

the croutons made the ballad—invalid—

INSTIGATE TO APPRECIATE

Once again I saw it then
                (and then) and then again
we defend the end they send
                        three feet from the repeat we treat as our own, out-
grown deformed reform.

Intriguing election
                pitting rejection v.s. affection
separates opposing states from common ground, with hands unbound,
with reasoning sound and
in its place losing the race shall descend 3 feet towards the repeat.

With odds of 10 to 1 there'll be no sun
                        the chance is takin', the limbs are breakin'
(in the middle of the middle) the bridge being bridle from emotionless action
and missing by a fraction creates a debate, so we wait for sunshine
                        while sitting on our ass
and dying of red wine
                in the middle of the middle
no thoughts, just riddles of primary colors
                        (us all being brothers) and actions taking
shape and fractions carrying weight on a bridge that sways in scary ways
knowing well enough alone the odds out-grown and our sun,
                        the sun.

TAKING A NAP ON THE INSIDE
OF A VEXATIOUS HYPERCUBE

and the headline reads:
*DRUGSTORE DRUID FOUND IMPALED ON AN INDIGO
HALLUCINATION*

the police investigate:
Crime scene; subliminal sanctuary
Prime suspect; immeasurable solitude
Motive; motivation
Eye witness(es); social backwash
Physical evidence; victims confessional
Time of death; victim survived

the confession:
i wish that i had written that song or could sing like that or play
some tune on any instrument, but desire and dedication march along
separate streets to separate beats. i would like to paint my dreams or speak
my mind or learn French or score 55 points against the New York Knicks
or grow my own tomatoes or dance or draw or be content with where i am
or what i do!!!

NOT the HERO TYPE

Come up Chuck, we'll discus the
disgusting
ebb and flow (and) the tide doesn't
know
what to where to a semi-formal funeral.

—

Patronizing patriots know none will

wait for us
to commence our defense
of the
flashback laughtrack.

—

Quiet King and Rook, saw the Bishop's book
on how the Queen and Knight killed the pawn
buried in the lawn
under the guise
of a semi-formal funeral.

EDITORS NOTE: An untitled work intended to be read internally with the reader secretly attaching their own title.

No partition between breeze and breath.
One shore lies under water's land step.
The same last name smiles all the while,
flesh and shore remain no more.

The image of a picture of darkness and light.
Pure perfect dream, bleeding wrong and right.
And after the now, now sends the end,
while darkness does break and light does bend.

Repeat the sound of isolated silence.
Knowing laughter is the opposite of anger's solo violence.
The purpose of the absence of a cloudy, rainy day,
explains the question of an answer washed away.

RESISTING PASSIVE RESISTANCE

The inscription on the throne is as follows:

ROMANCE INVADES LUST'S CREATION
SERIOUS EXPANSION REDIRECTS TIES
SOLITUDE INVOKES SINGLE SOLUTION
AND HERE IN THE CREATURE LIES
RESISTING PASSIVE RESISTANCE

The Emperor crowns the next in line
and the next in line will re-define
                    definition of the curse, the plague, the crime
while drenched in rhyme and backed by time
                    the thief and illusionist conjure commonsense
with psychokinesis and bits and pieces
                    of toxic beauty that's been hailed unruly, while
confusion is
refusing and resisting this thing denied, or rather defined as
                    passive and massive and
surreal;

                                        or bizarre
                                        or fantastic
                                        or grotesque
in time and in rhyme
being bloody from battle, with hand on handle and inherent facts of archaic
tracks
                    lacks the ultraviolet beaming of an entwined
                                        enzyme
                                            nightmare
wherein real fear may appear, but indeed
                    as always
                            here in it lies.

THE GREAT AMERICAN SHORT STORY

or: AUTHOR UNKNOWN

And so it was written. A complex look at a relative universe in the simplistic form of 'words'. An

original first draft from concept to creation the document embodies all that is true of art. From

hand picked and hand crafted, time tested expressions of liquid emotion perpetually unfolding, it

stands strong in the sea of misinterpretation. We are all critics.

Recent rumors to emerge on the subject suggest the unknown author to be a collaboration of

collective consciousness and unknowing participants. Some so-called experts go as far as saying it

is authorless. Creation without creator riddled with *a priori* and nearly mystical double meanings.

Although non-experts seem to agree on the importance of focusing attention to the work as a whole,

rather than waste our limited energy attempting to be the first to give credit personally to the author

of THE GREAT AMERICAN SHORT STORY.

EYEBALL THING

"No expression not withstanding, nor forced to explain advanced and pronounced access, nor interior descriptions of ones self, or any self, revives immunity thoughts that may have decayed along with the past / along with that feeling of near volcanic stimulation and the squirting of molten sarcasm and the rumbling of a voice cracking granite, while keeping intact a frame appearing human, while floating in an opium dreamtank [(a representation of the containment of all answers possibly wanted, but more than likely just as necessary as the containment of the container) a reference to itself].

That unjust too-true-glue-rule reeking of untimely displays in black and white of pressure-points / pointing the center of distraction (knowing that) relief by distraction empowers the mind to consciously inherit symmetrical resonance, gliding forward, seeming natural (and frictionless) masks resistance assuming automatic response technicians observe organic transfer of dream and sleep and night to assure accurate interception of realism, as it applies to those aware and un—, before and keeping within tangible existence and unreal expectations.

Semi-pronounceable, re-enforceable, fast-acting sentences seem to compromise compositions composed of absence absolute all the while spherical speculation re-defines reaction.

simplistic

delicious

eyeball thing

WHERE GOES THE GHOST

Naked and cool the need. Got ta have. All *calm* wants is nothing. A season inside yourself with independently moving, gelatin covered thoughts that say less for the need in all assumptions raining and cascading down upon desire's daydream. All *comfort* wants is nothing. No reason comes from within. No reason comes from the man with dark sunglasses who beckons the lady to look into his eyes. She resists and loves and dies and lives and loves every second that she is with him. Tapping the cigarette, tapping the table, tapping the brain, tapping the glass/the leading pain reliever (make that 2) in sample rays—shaded days—lazy ways believing all in which comfort wants. Comfort and calm were caught in bed together, wanting nothing of each other. Incorporating their past wonders into that same dream they both had while still lying in bed. Together. Naked and cool. This time it seems different, different than the last and the last of that. Stacked on top of one another; the days, the times, the experiences (that is) were stacked on top of one another, not calm and comfort. They did it doggie-style.

The further the days the further the ways. Independently moving, gelatin covered thoughts arriving at the same time, on opposite sides of the tracks. "JUMP. Dive, jump, jump now. Shit, now, do it now," yells the thought who wouldn't even give it a go.

"No patience left in that size, how about angst leftover from sexual tension? Something like this?"

"No. No thanks. It's just not me."

Well rounded, delightful sightings with intent on stress/stressing the diaphragm causing syllables to exit through exhale while riding on sound. A cute little identity crisis is forming around the burned edging. Crispy even. Live and direct, from 'he who greets with fire', comes passion and beauty just playing the part // falling a part in the dim light of a $55 story. Warm. Humid and delightful, well rounded. All the major food groups. Burning. Warm. Warm mix of air conditioning, country cocktails, burning, smoking little white pills together. In bed together they were caught. seen?

Heard. Alone in a room. Naked and cool. Cool because of the nudity. Nude without a garment which protects from sight that which was caught in bed. Together. Lusty and sensual, or consensual. They just met, in a bar, a saloon, a back wall watering-hole quartered and numbered and boxed in the strategic position of the drink as to force occasional eye contact. He was wearing dark sunglasses. He tapped the table. He tapped the cigarette. She'd rather not look to him. Not while anybody could see her that is. She'd rather it be our little identity crisis. She tapped the glass.

Only wants and needs. Wants and needs, needs and wants. Only wants need know needs want to know. The likelihood of a possibility looms on our event horizon. Relaying blackhole rising where exists that, which all was lost, before / in the first place to look was where stubborn people tend to say, "Nope. Not me. Not a chance. Not this way. Not today," softly to themselves as if whispering into the ear of a lover covered in sweat. Hot. Absorbent. Radioactive. Independently moving sweet sweat. Barely tolerable; the heat, the sweat, the movements a dance as a dance a need to cool off, to be cool. And naked. The possibility of a likelihood of a naked and cool, well rounded, delightful, ...

Caught in bed. Together. They didn't pay it no mind, just kept right on . . . . (nobody told) Sweating out the day, sweating out the booze, the present, the dim light of a 55 dollar story as if nobody (no body) would see them, smell them, read the story, turn on the lights. Higher, more wattage for fuck sake. Casting out shadows from the corners of the smoke laced room. The fifty-five dollar room draped in dim lighting which hid from notice; a bar area, a tape-recorder, a bible, a dictionary resting under the bed, listening as they contemplate profound aspects of humanity. "Is it in our nature to cause harm without fore thought? Do we really 'deserve' anything??" Red-winged Black Bird Blues is the tune on the radio. Real desire. Real daydreams. This is really happening, right in my own home, insects flying up to the screen. Let them out, how did they get inside. Let them out, who let them in? Get them high, so high, an insect flying, bites me at night. I at least own the good sense to pass-out, so I'm not up all night itchin' and scratchin' the marks left by the high flyin' insects that arrived without invitation, without warning, but not totally unexpected that is, since they procreate in any standing water which happens to be ever present. Still. Calm. Cool. Water. Ever present. Unseen, religiousless, mathematical daydream of a ghost. Ever present, tangible, translucent gravy, foglike substance. Lying in bed together, talking of the person who died on the couch in the 'living-room'. Il y a douze ou quinze ans de cela, mais je m'en souviens mieux que d'hier. (It is 12 or 15 years since that, but I remember it better than yesterday.) Dead. Three days on the couch. Permanent mark on the arm of the couch where stomach acids in his vomit ate away at a small portion of the upholstery. Police broke open the door after three days. Lock still doesn't work. Never got fixed. Never bothered to fix it. Too high, lying in bed together, talking of his ghost, tapping the cigarette. Not once reflecting on the $55 story. They were caught in bed, but nobody, no body said a word, not two words, not three . . . . Soon it wouldn't matter. Why bring it up? Why dig it up?? Ever present from a certain point of view. Perspective. Relative to where you're standing, or lying. Together. With a ghost. In bed. Unafraid, unhappy, unwilling after three days to get off of the couch! They had to break open the door!! Three days, now that's stubborn.

Better that yesterday I remember it. Probably because yesterday wasn't all that interesting. I was in bed all day long. So much so that I began to sleep on the floor when I desired sleep thinking sleeping thoughts of daydreams at night. Where goes the day? Where goes the story?? From here.

SEATBELTS ARE FOR SUCKERS

(introduction)

... then came the rain ...

*"It is the road of every Christian Man, who starts from the senses,
who is endowed with reason as a dialectical principle which, in
the drama of his earthly life, must make a decision between ever
increasing participation and eternal defection."*
—Erich Auerbach (Dante, Poet of the Secular World)

Begining and ending somewhere upon the brow of a day. Beginning
and ending somewhere inside the brutal, choking grip of Lake Superior's
winters, while dancing through shadows of everybody else's bad dream,
the brush strokes a numbing portrate of a selfabsorbed, socialy retarded,
artistic type of a half-human, half-poem, half-heartbeat. An abstract painting
with words (on the canvas of neurosis). No plot, no story, only conflict
unresolved and characters assumed.

*"All that he does seems to him, it is true, extraordinarily new, but also, because
of the incredible spate of new things, extraordinarily amateurish, indeed
scarcely tolerable, incapable of becoming history, breaking short the chain of
the generations, cutting off for the first time at its most profound source the
music of the world, which before him could at least be divined. Sometimes in
his arrogance he has more anxiety for the world than for himself."*
—Franz Kafka, "HE" (Aphorisms)

A diary of the id, dominated by the pleasure principal and paranoia,
irrational wishing and the immature evation of everyday life.
UNDAUNTED, I am my own distraction. Just another day and ALL being
still is well.

A tiny liquid blue box (holding all words never said) rests uneasily atop the bottom of a cliff. An 'actual size' roadmap leads to a land where sand can't be felt, felt can't be worn and wind wears away ocean sized thoughts / thought of previously, but never said, so night-time can unfold as told [with little to do of the day (as it only gets in the way) while magic and motion renew delight] none seem all and all seems right.

Beginning and ending underneath yesterday's monologue, (all words never said) underneath tomorrow's morality, (everything that shouldn't be done) underneath the clouds that are today, (awaiting the rising of the sun) . . . then came the rain . . .

PART ONE

(. . . and ALL seems right)

Feb. 13, 1996

I just don't know what to do with myself. Words / works from my past to begin being complete(d), work in the present to accept and future shock to blindly insert my creativity into a wall outlet, taking 220 volts just to get me excited. My knowledge of self—and its surrounding environment actually appear to double every 29 1/2 days and not only do I now dream in color, but I'm falling in love (again) with the sweetest of the sweet. Add a dash of springfeaver and a pinch of the (late)mid-winter *blahs*, bake at four-hundred and 20 degrese for an arbitrary amount of time, let cool, then dump it all on top of my hatless head. (Makes one serving).

Feb. 15,

UNDAUNTED

Feb. 18,

Must have blinked or somethin'. Once again days slip by like wet ice on wet ice, but not to fear / fearing not as I have narrowed down the cause of time's warping (unbeknownst to Albert E. I've created my very own) reasons; as day, roll over itself, trying to, it, self [(pass itself) with every cloudy exhale. Precise choise, strictly defined, mixed in moderation // I generaly don't mix] to punch through the E8 X E8 superstring theory formulation I recomend. For those who are sick to death of all the confusion I suggest . . . .

Feb. 19,

Winter, placing us all under the same glass cage and observes our (un-)dramatic reaction, as we watch eachothers and our own. Only Winter pays constant attention to detail.

Feburary 20, 1996

Pressures / left and right. Contradictions // Reactions (natural and controlled). Brail dominoes cutting lines for boundries of the court where the game is never always played all too, all too bad I've dremt this all before and should have written it down then. That is why, why ? "P.S., P.S.S., P.S.S.S.!

Feb. 21, 1996

Just another day.

Feb. 23, '96

Please, please, please another beer, imported please. A bowl of green from Bowling Green, soon to be orange, later than Sooner to be Oklahoma gray. Tired of Gin, Gin's tired of me. Please, Tennessee, please match mish-mash sourmash. A night. without M. is a blink, paused on pause. There's nothing wrong with white wine and pasta at night / a night like tonight another night. (and then another day)

Feb. 24th

Valued utilitarianism. Personal time (alone). Spells so strong that I *now* believe that I'm begining to comprehend people's grand stew that *now* we make when combined and left alone (together). Still, small talk and euphemisms give me a headache, frontal lobe. The patience of ten men with nothing to look forward to can not deny (can I) that the slightest detail of my existance is quite as plesant and joyful (I'm sure) as no other time in my woeful, smudgelike life. 10 years from the ground to zero.

Feb. 25, 1996

In the driver's seat, car in neutral, thinkin' 'bout walkin'.

Feb. 26,

Today. today happened. nothing more nor less, in expression, is a worthy sendoff into the annals of history than is the drying of cement already mortered and leveled.

Feb. 27,

feb. 28.

Feb. 28,

Same, except different. I'm fillin' in my costly freetime with higher thoughts and the quenching of a numbing thirst, instead of writing. I wish, (so do you) I wish it were different, but it isn't (it is just) // just the same, except different.

3/2/96,

Winter's subjects, labrats, cacooned prisoners of an eventual, eventuallity. Beyond the madness of (self, truth) shall come to pass. Eventually. Effortless patience brings the butterfly, eventually.

March 3rd, 1996,

. . . and ALL is well . . .

3/7/96,

Eleven cookie cutter, paperdoll, rerun, blah, rollover, blah, bland, blah, againagainandagain, days in a row, in a row, in a row . . . and ALL is well.

3/16/96,

Smokin' the weeks away. I'm convincing myself that the spring season will renew energies needed to have a creative summer. Until, enjoy (why not?) solitudesexslumber.

3/20/96,

Alex P. pointed to the heavens, M. and I looked upward, spring brought a comet. A comet brought spring.

4/7/96,

Between spring and Easter? (strategy-self)

4/8/96,

Focus / sucofnu. extend energy field evenly outward, beyond bodyglove fit.

4/9/96 or 4/10/96 (not really sure),

It seems and/or has just dawned upon me that it's more than slightly unfair (to myself) to attempt a summation of the events, thoughts, interpritations, reactions of any and all days (that I can recall). Unfair to the day, now that I think about it, not my sorry, drunken ass. I carry the wisdom and impression of each life lesson into each new day. The day, however, encompasses so much more than can be captured within 100,000 homespun journals [(without even trying.) I'm attempting to justify my drugaddictedlaziness. Perhaps if I were any kind of writer I'd . . . . aw fuck it. I reflect on the past quite abit these days. It kindof keeps me from worring about the future. I don't live in the Now, as I believe I should. I evolve into Zen states of maturation, Where Thought Is.

24 hours latter,
I'm dancing in the streets! Juke joint #2405. ("DAMN, if you weren't married, I'd be a cheater again.")

April 13, presunset:
Must elevate, must continue elevating, must remain elevated. Staying high (*stonedonanything*) about ten years in a row, in a row, in a row, fearing nothing but sobriety itself.

Almost April 15th,
ALL MOST APrIL 15, all most april fifteenth, AlL mOsT aPrIl FiFtEeNtH, but not quite.

April 21, 1996
Life continues to amaze and remain interesting enough to stick around. Wish you weren't here.

April 23, '96
When putting thought into word becomes difficult,

April 25,
Admit or rather realize, with every passing day I am finding a peace inside me that seems to have been there all along.

Authors Note: Looking back through the ages, through the pages— the April 25th and the May 16th entries caught my wandering eye. The three some weeks inbetween are where impact, upon distraction's basement floor, reached its maximum devistation. A nauseating ride on a caducean rollercoaster sponsored by "the apathetic—osterage effect" and all of the old favorites; morphine, codeine, demerol, alcohol (can't forget the booze), caffeine abused, marijuana & mushrooms, hashish & LSD25 (blotter-gel tabs-sugar cubes-liquid-on a piece of whole wheat bread), opium (not enough), cocaine (too much), marinol, methamphetamines (noun. a white, crystalline derivative of amphetamine, $C10H15N$, used in the form of its hydrochloride.), dexedrine, valume, ephedrine, riddelin, nitrus oxide, cough surup, (paranoia, lost hope, lost gaze, no clarity for me from here on out, untill the "Silver Ballad" reverberates). To me there's no between for I remember little except that many of the drugs were free, my body never left North America and Burroughs explained it all better.

May 16th, 1996 *Aboard the Demeater:*
  Repition smothers truth (ain't that the truth).

5/20/96,

6/3/96,
  Forgot (5/20/96).

6/24/96
  Ya just had ta be there, [(here). words restrict—event becomes image—end 'o story].

9-9-96
  I don't think that it matters that I lost my journal as a day by day, semi-strict and accurate account of the MAJOR and minor events that shape my persona and surrounding environment (which I in-turn shape) proved to be unreasonable for me. Alone together—excited lazy—sleepyson.
                              Keeping in touch,
                              —Ralph Waldo Emerson
P.S. it was under the couch

9/?/96
  I noticed March's entrie(s) calling for a creative summer. Poor, poor, Mr. Winter. Wrapped upinitself. Unaware of Summer's bloated and sweltering chaos.

9/28/96
  Leaf turning turns me green inbetween, turning foreground back and color. less.

10-?-96

Some strange change changing same strange change. ALL TOGETHER NOW. That's what **I, me,** was trying to say. Say; Stay, Now, Go. At least **I, me,** get it.

10-29-96

As luck would have it, births rebirth of confidence for years was never so near.

11-1-96

Ya, what (10/29/96) said!?!

11-2-96

That weight solid wait, noose intense mouthgag, incriminate and weight, tight noose mouthgag tight and tired! Expression mouthgag, thing tired, WHY SHOULD I? Not, why should I express incriminating solid wait, tight mouthgag? seemingly impossible for real, real, real, real, real.

11-3-96

High in the Afgani. hills; amist smoke, mirror(s), heat, Brutal revival of ex-sabitions (one act) solo, tribal, tempestuous corrections denied and held high amist smoke and mirrors. Trained in the art of survival of the sly(est) as they come and they're going anyminute, everyminute, every second a moment. "The moment of the murder, the moment of the kiss," to pass on solo, tribal, information accepting genuine genius. Looked down upon, talked down too, mismisunderstood. Protection from confusion high in the hills (ASMODEUS, deamon of lust) my guide inside.

11-?(4)?-96

Reconfiguring archaic, yet not that quite aged, vile in overview (quick overview) real (not so);quetasonfieguevisountatrae. Too two 2 real, seeing the darkness and the ease of which one can adjust to the lack of righteous acts and the adjustment to the darkness and the cumfort encompassing all and the murkiness wearing ones skin as a coat hovering the flesh; but *denying the fear,* the elements, the emotions, the feast upon algophobia and conscious dictation and reprieval of origionality prefered by non-creationism (ist). No non-belief revival.

11-(5 or 6 or 7)-96

It was the next step, save the choise of stagnation and hardly a step backwards is possible. It's that easy. "Death is no escape."—Jeff Walker.

11-7-96

Independent screams, garbage and other fine products showing English in 3-D to be a good enough method for the release of the hostage. Stay awake / staying awake to keep the vomit down, orinits place. Inconsiquential, speratic, calculated nonsense.

11-10-96

. . . and ALL being still is well . . .

11-11-96

Drunken carcass, meatlockers, hooks through lips. These are a few of my favorite things. No-no-no. I ment to say; "I'm drunk, listening to CARCASS, my home (different once again, after leaving M., after switching jobs, different once again, home / house // nails + wood = a shack) is as cold as a meatlocker and the anguish of aprehension shoves titanium hooks inthroughandout my purple lips." That's what I ment to write, but most of the time I shrink thoughts down to the size of their origional impuls . . .

. . . recovered in mid-flight, (no call was close) no hashoil can lubricate my cock, my joints. No taste melted cocaine ($C17H23NO4$) spits speed shine on my boots. No night greeted opium dreambox at the door, no love left in my heartbox for nooneno.

11-12-96

A dream so vivid (graphic colors, distinct smells, sounds and such, so) vivid I wondered where I was and if it was taking place in dreamland (part sexual, on the wing of a plane, woman on top, somebody I've never been close to intimate with, how 'bout that?). It was my awakened fealing; a sensativity to the ordinary, sub-conscious, one-act play that made me question the vdirseiaomn. Fully alert (?) and awake, the deciding vote v.s. emotionstate as was once was.

11-15-96

Too early to tell. Too late to take my place. Too, four, sex, ate.

11-20-96

Sleep tell lone for lone by self 'till self for sleep. Highly sexual antics. Fucking several different women at singularly different times and I still awaken alone (ain't that the shits?)!? One on the wing of a plane. Still dreaming the future, just paying it no mind.

11-21-96

Message from dream doctor Smithinsmith: "All is all is on call," said dead 'H' head. Back to Dr. Smith: "I ain't never druged a scare that met me."

Keepin' in touch—ralph waldo emerson

Early in the 11-22-96

Point after point makes it pointless. Desire indifferent. Dreamscape intake, the remainder / a portrate. The I, a mask, the we never demands such blowtorch type demands since scene now dead inbetween, but desire fades, hip weighters fill, mask drowning full, lone. night, lonetype, lone life lone. Just burry me in a warm, soft, tiny bed, dreaming self-inflicted, twice baked onlooker looking for once thought, twice infected brain scan. I mean . . . . I understand . . . . I know . . . . I want . . . . I am, I am not / / well deserved, well rested, welldone. Repeat threepeat we treat to the undone—did run—fun gun (fun, so fun) so I'm alone as I cryout just to hear me. Poor (poor) we.

11-22-96 still, later, still awake days later

I'm serious, this little shed that I call home is a fuckin' Croation meatlocker (but) I do prefer it over climate controlled complacency. I sit across from a mirror as I write. smoke. shoot-up. snort. sip. spell, bad speller listening to somebody different than the manchildman I notice observing me.

11-29-96

BLAH!! (into / blah) and LATER THAT SAME DAY, came soft warning: Welcome to the Monkey House. Please seat yourself. peace to Kurt V.

12-1-96 disolves into 12-6-96

through doors of windows and actual, fully colored, big screen, surroundsound, living, breathing, dying, loving, deflating, confusing, refusing, resolving dreamtime, daytime, sometime such as now. Washing down speed with Champagne, liquid smoke, liquid lunch, champagne brunch, absent munch, missing all not too much.

12-8-96

Unfolding headfirst, fullback through any block and tackel. Five or 6 just to take me down without the ball. Focus, stay, bloomBOOM. Bashing back headfirst. Oddmanout.

12-?-96 *Up here where the booze flows faster and funnier than the news:*

Up here in Northern, Northern Wisconsin winter does not approach. It declares War and Victory on the same day. Those that survive the innital assulte will be shelled by self; bombarded by bombs, driven intoexile, underground/indoors, forced to cope, survive at long last for 22 weeks of winter becomes 22 months of seasonless sundays (all the while reflecting on a hot sandy beach, with a cold beer and warm flesh).

Accept, flow, change, embrace, go swimming.

12-20-96 into 12-24-96

Inbetween, on a roll.

12-27-96

(. . . the anticipation of . . .)

1-1-97

I resolve to "Double the Dosage."

1-3-97

A kind of Crazy, Funky, Spooky, Dookey high (in color, in living, in Louisiana, insane). $200,000.00 "missing"/not missing, has to be somewhere.

1-6-97

An inky, stinky, callous void in place of an absent ultraviolent emotion. A quiet kill. A painfull suffacation, gulping, frozen vacume packed, airless airbagged air. A hash bash retreat, a promise in a lie in a thought (lies the future) in a thought / in a thought the future lies. "Time is told that it's better than gold," lie #1. Now to express exactly what I 'nvision; cold, vibrant fog and soon all is forgotten, all is prophetic, all is neuron sparks peakin' not speakin'.

1-7-97

We hate eachother, (ourselves) we tolerate eachother, we pay homage and love and curse and fuck and shun and plot against and rally around eachother, one another, everyday / questionmarks appear under footsteps, **this** moment forever **then**. Still I wonder not blushing, still common, sharing disasterous fantasies, fantastic footsteps and still.

1-8-97

I am my own distraction. Civil-eye-za-shun, with a double shot of whatever.

1-13-97

The missing words, they're not in here. da statue a limit a shuns, How weird, How antiapropos.

1-18-97

The test, the change, a handfull, an earfull.

1-27-97

drink Drink, drunk stoned, stone drink. This planet I will spare, this lust demon timeshare. REVENGE. My revenge, a voodoo dream cursed in all paths shining a hell to be taken lightly.

2-23-97

Serious freedom. Serious distraction woven into times unfolding, where experience fuels its own needs and wisdom is gained in specific chunks of freedom (this being one) . . . . Murder all the great. High to say, "*LSD* spray," Operation Artichoke: BZ gas (U.S. Army's Super *LSD* in spray form) . . . . I can't find the time to brush my teeth while zombieing around in my fully awake, Mescal dream. I think I'm violently intoxicadrunkated.

2-27-97

Creating moments converging on a fork (and the TAO jumped over the moon).

3-5-97

Get the point!?!

3-10-97
Oh, fuck it, you had to be there!

3-12-97
A friendly reminder,. and that's the good news.

3-13-97
True enough, behind the 8-ball, benieth the wheel, in control,
independent salvation, orgonized chaos renered harmless, spastic speedline,
passive panic, wideawake, dead tired, running from, going, falling upward,
ditch digging, sead planting, flower smelling, drunken clarity, cloudy
notions, best intentions, worst outcomes.

3/24/97
And again the spring, again a comet, without M., without Alex [r.i.p.
(without a reason why)].

4/15/97
Once again.

5-?-97
Unreal as all is.

6-2-97
I died as I lived, nothing more said

8-25-97
To kill, to be kind, fractured words, out of time. Diabolical / Evil //
Incantations.

9-3-97
,oh my died and dies as life stands in the corner with the coroner,
nobody's looking. Typical unrest; kicks in (in seconds), flexing, checking
windows, cuming spastic ballpoint soft joints, lovin', savin' time,
disintegrating ray of emobolization. Shock crazy zoo. Can't write anymore
wrong. unhook.

END of LINE.

PART II

(none seems ALL . . .)

"What's madness, but nobility of soul at odds with circumstance?"
—*Theodore Roethke*

10-?-97

The Pale India non-dairy lovelee cosmic percussion production, invites solvent secret serpents home with human creatures—face to face—for once and only—looks to be in all it is / only and once // to face the face [(facts and secret) silent] in-between problem and places puts paint and plaster before and always.

Berlin cries its milky dream. Black footwork, scorch-marks tagging the crotch of the retired sleeping cat burglar. (I stole 3 cats this month) . . . never did unfold . . . never fold / folding with 3 of a kind showing. That thought, being human in a non-dairy, skim sort of . . . GOD bless it all (in [all is] all) that was once and only a memory of a daydream, that same dream we have everynight, every Saturday night . . . sore hands, bad knuckles, been snappin' 'em ever since I'ze seven. Seven or 6 I forget. Forget or forgot (that dream). That's why it keeps repeating . . . and over and over perhaps I mean, even maybe I should try and write it down on paper and all . . . "The dream;" that is, on paper, repeating since I was six or 7 . . . face to face (with a serpentlike, nonhumanistic impossibility that snakes / slithers / slinks / away, representing itself as if, within, at all, being that itis such as much as in itself [(as any other who dreams or dares to *dream*, (Dreaming . . .))] Now . . . .

ENTER DREAM:

. . . . of. Satellite launchin' motherfuckers doin' just what I would've done if the grass wasn't so pale green at the bottom of the ladder, mast cells trembling on the other-side of our non-existent fence / fencing the swordplay, compromising launch codes, morning glories dreamin' a deamon box without socks in a black and white and read all over Muscat & Oman's daily tribune, blessing hot oil (not all to be unshown) received in layers // in that space between closure of a circle, arching as itself has close just to start anew. That point of predetermined nothingness. A predicting Pale Indian Voodoo Dream on paper and all that isn't (with a breath) and a kiss of nighttime air / seeming much less than that which becomes important, but perhaps in a fluid bleach madness with third person's fourth hand truths // riding a ripple, dropped on a moment in-between that space closing a circle. What went around came around, tarnished with time, inadequate remnant observers of the spin and velocity (one at a time ya know) is all that truth will allow according to the laws of Physics / handed down, written on paper, pulled from Berlin's chilly and moist, evening air. I should know. I was there approximately 240 years ago. They have changed; the times I get no time the years, but people (the same) years, as in tracks / keeping track of rotation(s) with them. The people / years // time can not change them as the same they "Stay." The people (us,we) we dream / us, ourselves (all together now) are autumns true colors; as in dream colors cover canvas, stiff and thick, while strange summer winds caress treetop's tiptop. The very top that birds and camera=crew's low-flying, government, unmarked, politicians see with high-resolution imaging satellite's / low-flying orbit over Berlin, or was that Tennessee??? // !!!

END DREAM.

Preaching evolution/evolving and revolving in circles on a spiral (x-y-z) to say the least is more than one can stand (or sit or lay) awake at night, stuck, daydreaming by the ounce; fluid, motionless, self-inflicted summer breeze // dropping leaves and branches and pinecone acorns, warm and full of sunshine in shorts, in my car, in October, in Lake Superior, in a daze /// catching rays, catching ways of waves of thought through out the years.

All them years starting over and over and again and over in a circle on a spinal fluid spiral. Valiant Guardian of daydream's snake chase. Wasting verbs in a soup, stewing and brewing classical shade tree [(Jefferson Davis Oak-Tree, Beauvoir Mansion Estate of Gulfport, Mississippi)

Editor's note: the word 'Mississippi' is both fun to write long-hand and to type.

over 500 years old / classic shade tree's seen quite a few full moons (six-thousand plus / 6,000 +)]. Quite a few rings in that trunk, a whole bunch of circles / all most all of them as a shade tree, Sir, General sir!!

Losing No sleep in "Friendly Manitoba" / well, only on purpose. Purpose on paper as it should have been before, on paper before (what was I thinking?)!, thinking of Tennessee, of lastnight's dream, of the purpose on paper and it's effect on being (as is not untrue) no untruth being thought (and/or) unstated will be taken' as given' being even giftwrapped in a 30 minute; dimensional and directional, wandering, magnetic, drawing towards and into the center of the(a)circle. A single point whereupon can stand, nothingness while occupied (as it always is) being as it is not untrue / No. Creating the ordinary from the fantastic, enjoying classic selections of negative occurrence / occurring something sort of mutual in respect, while complaining of the environment—curious—willingness—joking—commonly captive—traveling, low-flying whatever timeaddress continuing direct eye-contact (reaction) face (to face) serpent chase // troubled specifics /// experience carried on the other hand, developed independently company risks [agreed immortal (say "immoral")] well aware of terms, on variables, of intensive, in assessment sit-down strength, preventing model value . . . wholesale rotten secretes solution slipping silent impact and contradicts ignorant involvement in teaching imprint, abstract, pointless rules beyond behaviors example, between roles in trust and in reason. Living well, wasting verbs, throwing curves while getting all getting just what I deserve(d). I deserve October in Seattle, common traveling captive / joking willingly as the blushing bride, lacking pride, knows just where to sit. Driving force points the coarse of / of a now known to fit right, filling blank space with empty thought // thought out of sequence, piece by part by fraction with friction, on Comet, on Cupid, on Donner, Safety blitzin' linebacker coverin' the Flat Fat Tuesday [(easily the Big Easy Gulfport voodoo dream.) Fade to Dream . . . .

ENTER DREAM

. . . . pistol toatin', fraction floatin' blank place choakin' space, or that exact point in space closing a circle on a spiral [(x-y-z) Cartesian coordinates] at that exact moment, captured, satellite over Berlin; *Stellen sie das Radio an, Der empfang ist heute abend schlecht, Man be kommt nichts als Storungen,* . . . signal is picked up both in Zagreb and somewhere in the

[Colorado Mountains. (Panel watching, cigarette smoking', Virginia blend) CIA rolled it for the Sir, General Sir] . . . Now into a Belgian diamond nightmare / dreamtime wanting, made aware paid the fair and pulled the hair roots voodoo doll choking out of sequence, bleeding parts and pieces as Deamons feast upon frozen, faulty, facets of the Evil in Good // down wind of October's breath . . . Island time, treetops top o' the mornin'; quality time's national average peak performance / performing Show Business // Show Biz mangled bleach madness. As in . . . .

ENTER THE DREAM IN THE DREAM

. . . . Dear Diary,

You'll never guess what I did today!?! I was at the Kingdom in Seattle, swaying on the mainstage, accepting an award from a group of well established writers for being voted, "Least likely to succeed and less likely to care about it." While walking off-stage I spotted Noah Webster the sixth in the audience and yelled, "Hey, Webster, spell check this," the entire time holding my crotch . . . Backstage the food was prepared by the homeless, ex-cons to watch the kids, politicians jacking-off chemical company exec's while the media turns it's collective head to cover the African-American that just robbed the closest gas station because he was sick to death of being broke. The molested son of the neighborhood priest turns off the news to concentrate fully on the crackpipe / getting every last, flaky morsel // "Shit's expensive, ya know?!" His best friend, she's a little, white girl who whores on the weekend, she's 14 years of age (closet case, very sad). She keeps him informed. The best times, the best deals. He's had crack fever dreams of fucking her from behind while beating his father with a hammer until he lets him take the JAG. out for the evening (all night even), but that thought never crosses his daylight mind. Besides, she's only 14 and dad, he really does love me . . . The corporate lawyer is dabbling in Sin. The local Sheriff is rumored to be crazy, he's talking football with a Judge of somesorts. They make a generous wager and sip a drink on it. The Judge doesn't care of the wager all that much. He'll either pay the Sheriff from his bribe money or receive winnings from the Sheriff's stockpile of crime scene cash. He doesn't really care, he just likes to bet, makes the game a bit more interesting. The Sheriff doesn't care either / he's been drunk since four o'clock // he doesn't come off duty until the Kingdom is cleared and locked, he doesn't have time enough to care about the game, although he did find a few moments to escort me off-stage. I didn't put up much of a fight, I was drunk too. He showed me the parking lot then let go of my arm and shoulder. I turned to him and said, "That must be against the rules or somethin', eh." "Ya, it still is, least while the press is here," belched out Brandy from the Sheriff's mouth. "What's the spread on the 'Husky' game," I ask? "Don't know," Sheriff said turning and going back inside, "ask the Judge." (fade back to now) . . . .

END DREAM(S)

IGNORATIO ELENCHI: Ignorance of the refutation . . . . Sing a line . . . . Greedy, tragic, mystic maker / making songs sung with direct eye contact. Splendid years avoiding ?why? / that's nice, that's a stopspell and it's an afternoon in October and it's an incantation of sadness, choking trees // changing chaos into sweltering sounds of sleepless tribal chanting /// voodoo whispering tornado warnings continue to spiral acceptance (singing and sailing and trembling bricks) break the sleepless mid-afternoon into what it really is. Motionless. Proud, song dreamt of the night before / all this happened, before all of this . . . started over, circle anew, same-spiralself saw worse for ware warfare belief / convenient problem tied tight, night (afternight) daylight tree shaken' shade tree // leaves rustle on our evening' shade. Between the night and sunrise, the shadow dies. Participate in the experiment. Untimely Vodka Confidence, unashured silent style of flesh and information, worries and wastes nature, naturally undone / Necromancer avoiding eye-contact, greed taken for granted, accepted motionless less emotion rotation. Kind words console painless, timeless scrolls while a Pale India evening spent with a room full of strangers spinning strange conversation around a shelf (full to the gills) of bottle-glass-bottles. Quarter covers bowl / oxygen choked out of existence // clearer images strain the brain; great relief, breaking of the clouds, the room will empty, except for the impression of the collective emotional output (layered on the paint and plaster, woven into the evening, mixed with the drinks, adding to the ambiance, floating in the air, thick as cigarette smog).

Have I lost you? Are you not where we thought we should be? . . . . leading the blind, The Blind . . . . in the breeze / the breeze through the trees reminding me that I've dreamt this all before // me reminding me (myself) that I should have written it all down back then. *Before all of this.* Before that dream lastnight . . . .

ENTER DREAM

. . . . a lentil and rice gypsy King cab driver. He's from Haiti / He rolls past a building with the words, "Come Not Between The Dragon And His Wrath!"—W.S.

spraypainted in silver—black—crimson—blood—breath / He blinks— rolls past slow, rolling, wondering when and where building and breath and brick slowly rolls, rolling slowly past the past and into info., out through tagged trickling truth (in words) spoken or written or thought // dreamt. It all before (it all happened). It was Bill, Billy Shakespeare spraypainting the words, *"attendez-moi ici,"* on a back-alley wall facing Mobile Bay, overlooking the U.S.S. Alabama and its WW2 submarine accompaniment the U.S.S. Drum. Toured the south pacific I believe. (Big. Big guns covered in seagull shit. Billy found that image, oh so deliciously humorous.). I got lost once or twice while touring the Alabama's big . . . . BIG boat; the boat I got lost on, but felt rather safe, calm. Big, Big boat [(calm and collected the entire time as low-flying whatevers, shot down in the Pacific Campaign, or the Passive Campaign to be literal on paper) in-front of y'all] with a purpose in the correct direction / left to write, coast to coast, off to the left time left to pick apart // one on 1 express quick rhythm pattern's intense trickling truth. Mr. CabDriver expressing concern's return in words blasted!!! loud words returning concern. Undaunted. Reborn in scorn. Dark flashlight beam tails up and away while Show Biz bleach madness; whitewashed, backtapped adrenaline tank, overlooked it, ignored it, untouchable, unheard of It. Happening now before it all happened. Passive it all is now, Passive Campaign to be literal. "GO BAMMA" spraypainted on the side of spiraling coconut bark, palmed trees of the various conquered (liberated) island paradise, or pair of dice to be literal. 7—7 11, seven / eleven slow-motion rolls slow roll, rolling past spraypainted building walls decorated at the base with pushers, thieves and dopeheads, tossing a pair—of—dice at a wall directly underneath the word 'Wrath', painted with pleasure (and out of disgust). Haitian Cab Driver rolls past slowly, I'm in the backseat on my way to the bus station, or Hell, or East Saint Louis (not that E. St. Louis reminds me of Hell's classical stereotype, as it is much to cheerful). In my mind, out in the open I say . . . ,

"I'll never run through wet grass concrete fields again / Bulletridden newspaper drop-off, 'Paper's going to be a few hours late this morning, there's a hostage situation up the road blocking traffic. No—no—no don't

bother going back home, these things don't last long statistically speaking.'
We entered the scenario minutes into it; the subject (black and white and
read all over both switching on our downtime artistic hobby program)
being gray and overcast, more defined than I recall."

The entire time I had a head full of acid and was with a Giant softbox
subject willing to give the Northstar a chance, high in the Afghani Hills
amist smoke and mirrors. Interesting technique you use. Rookie of the
year called up from retirement, on a bookshelf old film rolls, rolling past
the past, slow, complicating things without even trying; all that hard (that
is) on the bookshelf / new books // old words on paper that should've been
written down years ago, before it all happened, before October I stopped
wondering IF and just knowing when I peaked in on the caramel separated
seabreaze to rewrite the retort / Carolina Report. Being seen, not heard,
with the sacred word walking hand in hand through the naked forest.
Wind blowing treetop branches falling in the fall forest scene. Sneaking up
on the past, in the woods you must be quieter than you think you are
thinking not hearing the sacred word being talked about amongst yourselves,
alone, walking hand in foot through the Carolina forest // leaf turning
turns me green in-between, turning foreground back and color less. Less
animal innocence seeming so primitive / spotting eachother, the noseknows
motionless captured sense of smell, startling momentary laps of courage
and conviction reducing itself to a lesser form of survival, seeming so primitive
that it appears to be the only way to reconnect bookshelf retirement, as it
is too touch minus with plus and see if sparks fly away // low-flying
foreground turns me green in-between, allowing re-entry of orbit and a re-
entry into a story taking place in this conversation *that's already in
progress* . . . .

END DREAM

Now, what were we talkin' 'bout, as in some abstract joint venture of a
Deamon teared trident and a hunter with a Smoky Joe, not that he's a big
fan of his wife's kabobs, he just enjoys the sound of meat burning fat over
an open flame. The sizzellsmellsound tickling his ears/nose/crotch/trigger
finger, at the sametime his wife runs back inside the house to fuck (get
fucked) the hunter's friend (quanta former friend). They did it on the
couch, over the arm of the couch, on the footstool infront of the chair, on
the chair, on the ladder leading to the loft, in the loft, on the bed in the

loft // He came back inside the house to get a gun or two because he heard a Deer or Elk or Moose or Aardvark or Tourist or something such as the sizzellsmellsound of sex. Forbidden fornication (with finger on trigger) he had to decide whom or what to kill. Something had to die, must die tonight. Why not him?! Well she's nobody to die for and 'friend', he just wanted her shapely shape and she, she just wanted someone besides the hunter and that Caribou outside had nothing to do with any of this.

Shit, something has to die tonight.

Why not my formed defense analyst's pure, perfect dream? "What," you say?!? A spastic type of geometric shapeshifting penny drop. Little is known, but the knowing, timetested bright best dehydrated, re-instated back hoe's backsores / no more interest in trust ing as it once were // was or is (isn't it refreshing while undressing the end) being more than the all > interesting in peaking the Why/How/Why Not/ When/Where/With Who or whom it may concern, concerning distaste and that taste in choice (knowing or not) of what will when win before and never again will win one more than the trust in-trust-ed to, too, also two and before for; the sun giving it a shot and once cold now hot, brilliant bright, warm October oozing through the song filled filling form after form (forming filled files) from bottom to top and some underground, missing nothing, no thing— expressin' *regretful replacement* (who left whom, remember!?!)?! Low ball, big hit, big boat, big guns, big little big / gone to the dogs as they miss no thing. Radio sports tested and guaranteed annoyance of saw and tool merchandise glassware weather labwork functions beautiful and efficient, catching quiet lead-off / back-up deceptive imagery divided by totals ever written recordings of every individual singsong expression ind impression that I receive is the impression you put out / give-off / give up for free at all cost to yourself, charging none that will misssee, mini-misinterpret corporate coaxing of the (sir) General (sir). Public intoxication in an unreliable foreground casting molten deadline time change; redirecting indirect directions, pouring into plaster casting maintains composure underneath the weight of wait // gone to the gods as they miss nothing!
Patchwork brainscan guessing guesses / living frivol, wind loves wine workers toasting our sins, sampling our dreams with bluecheese and animal

crackers, fermenting that thought last thought we had just before we wrote
our poem, before we punched that undercover cop, before we got on the
7:55p.m. bus, (going from 'old' Seattle to Greenwood and 85th, to sing
three rounds of Yellow Submarine) before we stole that $40,000 Cadillac
just to go and get even drunker, screw some college girl in the front seat,
take it back and piss on the tire. Wind loves wine workers without sins of
there own / tasting and disliking // disliking, but knowing what is accepted
as good or classy or vibrant or valuable patchworkmissing, no think, no
thing maintaining invasion's impression expression of written records of
actual thought [(electric muscle moving impulses imposing in press ing
upon the paper) ink slime] little big gone / deadline // *molten distraction*,
such as . . . .

ENTER DISTRACTION

. . . . I like to pretend that I do not exist as an afterthought of public
discrepancy wrongly chronicling the France romance. I betray composer's
composition / compiling headfirst, out gunned (big guns), outnumbered
numerous nullified transcontinental orbital shift. Funding for the majority
will be found in a West Coast Federal Bank, "them bastards, so that's where
all the money is," isn't hid in (when it is then) it will not be in average
short supply; cells divide, as downtown Havana has my complete attention,
preserved in a jar by that Haitian Cab Driver / daring to respond, involving
opening ties // ties news towards freemarkets (knowing the nose still knows
what is losing is lost in touched discoveries /// discovering; poems to make
you blink—poems you may or may not understand—poems and
headaches—poems with a beer chaser—poems to make you say,"uncle!"
The first word in last words, craving an audience of unmasking,
nonunansewerable nauseating question, less reception. Intriguing and
exciting (saying more without a soundsave skull sanctuary) and believing
and dreaming and living in total control. Spotlight walker with shadow
choking reflex, central nervous system of intelligence agent's soft
contactlense's satellite questionless reception. Seadplanting, spreading the
b.s., covering selfincased warmth coated nitrogen. Storyteller's sad spell;
sad numerous tale teller told first in the third person, second in only seconds
and finally never final / finished written records of actual patchwork, needle
maid // maid and played in real time, reel to reel, feeling to feel—
unappealing appeal pulled apart, first at the start, second in seconds and

finally undone. It is not the way we do things, it is the way things are done / unknown cover covering contradictions in life and love long being that feeling once let go. Never sit still, will willing thrill, thrilling blowtorch (jaw driven, licensees, freelance treestance) bleeding verbs, smudgelike ink running words laced with PCP and left-over (past) a paper teaser / teasing 'till individuals cursed with hollowed points pointing crushed, unique exit-wound, existing alternative names of trusties covering lax-trax while news breaks into bits (it's buried into a false flag sting operation; unamused innocence, tools) of the trade formulating opinions, expressing regret and repressing some untold timebomb. From now on it is I that will be filled with massive and passive no, none, nothingness, not you / You (and all of yours). Speaking out of turn, turning the wheel (circle) navigate the spiral (x-y-z) AND hope AND pray AND vomit acoustic colors / magnetic refreshment dispenser. Semi-interesting new look / looking dry, smokeless play change interference. Toothless (loose), stinking biohazard on edges edge (less) timeline, not known to soothe smooth nerve endings ending dazed days and gray sky ways. Wine and dine lentil and rice gypsy King cab Driver. A true worldproof 9millimeter generation generator, cranking ampere soup and a treetop seabreeze story. (story) Greyhound and All Hallows Eve, blizzard bastard on the out and / out of Fargo, chainlinked tires tripping thin ice shaved snowcone, coconut flavored lipstick tasting a hooker named Brandy, dancing—lapdance to Mr.Brownstone // limp, boozeless reaction (escaping to maltliqure hotelroom, watching Indiana vs. Charlotte, passing out—cold). Now, that's much better.

END DISTRACTION

Lost in a motherfuckin' world of sadness, madness is all that was once, all that blood drips a circulation and isn't what once was. Never making it (it being made) to 25 as twenty-five is. To see blood / bleed, precious drop by drop to death being done and gone. If anything was to be said it wouldn't be overheard, as if heard not feeling feelings once had. That mix-and-match emotion potion felt while sitting alone in my car; I coasted into the driveway with the lights off. She was in the house / home capital A frame rented // rental, I could see her, I just finished a thirteen hour shift (holiday day spent butchering cold, blood-soaked, glandspewing beef + chicken + pork + fish + lamb), she worked before sunrise baking underpaid, unappreciated, sweetened sweet treats. I hadn't been with her in hours and hours and days and ages. I could see her through the window glass moving about, as I sat in the $1,000 car letting that creamy, electromagnetic feeling of daydream and desire swirl within my chestcavity; picturing myself running up to the door, stopping, catching my breath, opening the door and taking her about the waist, allowing that feeling I held selfishly to spew so strongly from my fingertips, sparks would singe her homemade dress. But instead, I sit in the car, smoking a bowl of weed that I can't afford and drink strait Gin from the bottle I stole until that something, that whatever. fades into . . . . while still knowing not what knowing cares, caring away, still far as gone is. Unimpeded through thin and thinner thickened thoughts, thought of once and tossed away, still far gone / gone and once, I think. Preserving precious patented patterns, formulate distant numberbox names, burning solo wanting seeds, believing hammerhead's total timebomb. I let her go as she let me go as we slipped away as I pushed her. away.

My global economic meltdown / quake cracking crackdown (felt feeling transparent), jumping the passive Pacific, snitch-snicker-curse, worse than Mr. Jones dancing on the angles angels on the head of a pin / pins and needle's needle exchange // rearrange the sentence [(25 to life) tools as art]; instant objection, general public, Sir, General, sir saw the sea scene, mobile contraption moving up mandarin side, movie head ex-exec. added and padded and pounded nail after nail after spike after drink after drink, before and after sir saw sea scene still knowing *none of the above* as being true to my words written sad spoken thoughts /// thought of being bound to action. Acted upon as is and isn't, "stimulus seamless dressing regression's repression obsession," as wind worn back-tax bleeds black and white / right and might be the wrong song sung as swans dance with vultures, minutes tick time off // away to the Future new.

Back to the basics, back to the boomin', bumpin', funk trunk, holdin' most security away with an axe / the battle-axe battelin' rats rattelin' right wordless left. What remains but dried out brains, hang-man hanging onto a dream I've never had, in a place I've never been to // too two (twice) spoken, once thought and always known for 4 or once more being been and now is to come with a headfirst and foremost is the most, more than all (or most of all) thought they knew new evolution revolution solution being as simple as the problem / slash / concept that was brought into existence by those that knew and he who did, being he who is (isn't) always and forever *and ever and* and and . . . .

. . . . oxygen homecare, impossible reduction honing sonic soundscape, acid reflux rotting ribbons received at random, eventold everlasting eventuality of chaos masking manic magi's marbled mouthful. Synthetic superstring, twisting turntables, old fables and soup labels at random, impassable and everlasting timeshare / homecare medicine head. Like the darkness between what we knew and how for four tenths of 3 seconds, clocks stand still, waiting for the seven thirty-five bus that never arrives late, but is always on time / of its own making new rules out of aged, misshapen, redeformed affirmations // six fold concentration, red on red, claw tooth headhandle hidden from the dark, day-time at the park, trailing flashbacks through the unknown plains of existence as random as. Not feeling selfseeing WE, being of sonic sound mind and body decay; rapid mass transit authority figures fucking the rules, tiedying the schools, believing the fools. And war having its say and tunes evolving in a way (of our past to come) in present tense unsung confidence. Speaking from the ethereal plain surrounding round, all around as is and always (the slow chosen doom or sane or walking thin) pounding, pumping heart (crash) / (thump) 2—3—4 the rightway. Hostile profile denial, playing not the dog solo scramble as all, not known, is unlisted old news!)?; what's wrong with correct mistakes? Dead when confronted, appearing less daunted (un) than caring is to notice all that's been done as such a goodboy / playing nice / throwing dice / Cab Driver spotting me a twentybill. Fairness fair-weather warning 'll see never works in this galaxy again once again, as again, medicine head (with body parts spread over 15 states) 2 countries contradict, poisoning saneself supposed primal concrete spike, sewing sacred seeds of flesh and blood and health and feeling the feeling you've never had while wide (open), wide awake, but sleepdreamt of it happening in a super sphere of sound and trouble.

Trouble sleeping less wondering aloud in sub-zero silence coating 3:00 a.m. in a hazy glow of color and fiction. Westward reaction defaces proud cloud-dancer, while the driven springsong knows sunrise could take long, to close and open chapter and verse on subject and predicate. Crystallized fortunes resold and unfold before sleepless eye's terrible demise. The new sun's rays and sweet Jane sways as cloudmass / thunderblast down from up on high, reading nights old, simple sky. Shadowcaster re-dreams my last thought taken out of context in full view of our present, the (now)'s sadshape two-tone blank stair. Speaking soft, breakin' in places and parts, singin' soft so feeling uneasy with reason and rhyme, some on the time, thinking needs / and still dancing, but sees not sais, just is and does. The (now) sat still when it really should have been liquid, in motion (forward), causing, doing, making from the stuff of nothingness (known to be shaped into anything). Not still; so no circle's pointless point, pointing less and less, re-dreaming that last dream, the one where I had trouble sleeping / three o'clock antemeridian (*trois heures / du matin // Ca prend combien de temps?*). Prodigious times standing tall, being stuck as psychological profile controlled, absorbed indeep, before the face of all—of—this cloudless sunsets series restricted // how's the view"??" Fallen' behind reminds confident consistence containing cosine of x-y-z while singing same sad song, overflowing into lazy (lessness) more say no, now and then needle twitch seems same still same / equal to basic chanting songs lost inside without having to cum [out, (outside it is)] it's overwhelming—to know travel time beings, being (been) *done and gone . . . .*

The South and the Silver Ballad

. . . . so far the silver ballad reverberates only inside of circles and spheres, while back on Physical Earth. Well rested, damned and tanned in sequence, counting on winnings counted before the eye blinks (faster than the hand) on a Wet and Wild Gulf Coast Voodoo Fantasy / Hardwood profit // Micronation sunsation soaked in booze and plenty o' animal flesh grillin', super saturated soil, all thought unaccounted for. Clean slate, shavin' and behavin'. Semi-sober subtle rebuttal (force fed false facts) appeased with corkdriven; unforgivin', relivin' same old unnoticed noise maker. Scattered skull, thought driven overload, linking Old Scratch to rumor and fact and to hard nose tact, (un)believing bleeding and receiving fermented shock-treatment. Administered sinister stealer, taking yesterday (hier) from those who don't mind it missing. And so all can be undone. My 725th (siebenhundertfunfundzwanzigste), time undoing yesterday so near to today / sets no regret as we believe we wash away into a homegrown silver song / / singing over and over in our heads, "What they knew they thought, we knew was said instead." Nothing can return to where it once was—all change writes strange stories of clowns and fools—the times, ten times, Zen rhymes and wades hip-deep in selfish ways. All truth is why I exist and no lie can blame resist. My God I will forgive, my future in pictures taken by blinking, shaking and shrinking into subcompact portable photons and positrons.

Even this (which was always so neat and sophisticated and comfortable and righteous and known to be the way things are done) can collapse upon itself in a most bizarre fashion, including and up to the very point in which everything was set-in-motion. The undefinable position in my vacuums packed vortex, in the indivisible matrix, in an all encompassing reality known by none other than ALL + one / everything ever done and thought, trapped and living, so lifelike, in the center of absolute nothingness. Our concept left alone / left and right // right and wrong just is not the point, our point in space, a space unseen (set in stone) for the first and last time timeless to say we always knew an action should be taking shape. Points on a powder line, curving into itself. A hypercircle is its own creator and it's seemingly as enigmatic as water dripping onto the grass, into the soil, into my cloudless, multicolored sympathy coating lesser known lies. There are just more reasons not to feel the Earth rotating (an excuse for almost everything); a pain to fry, a death to die, a bead of sweet posing as a droplet of water, clinging to the outside chance of becoming a trailblazer, unique in all surroundings / surrounding itself // ourselves /// another one another wonder where, wondering how things went wrong. But that isn't the point . . . .

. . . . near the end there is a point in which all words touch and no touch feels . . . .

February 11, 1998

Dear diary,

Today I spotted my first Georgian rainbow. Gravity's disconnection (hollowed and crystalline) with that which it attracts; being natural and seeming forced / forcing twilight onto shadow where there once were bones, dead bones rolling comfortable circles down simple sprinkles of what was known. Making one last stop, the same as it ever was / observing faces in visions of patterns and impressions. Unable to shake, can't stop all nonsense decoded, can't resolve plastered pain and supersensitive energy reception. The challenge of gravity, under the murky chaos surrounding everyday rotation on an axis central point, remains to be documented or believed or even concentrated on for more than a moment (the same—very same moment that forces twilight). So the PULL, acceptable in its simplest form, being quiet unto itself, knows no alignment / bleeds no excuse // suffers collective judgment and pays it no nevermind. Branches of rootwords relive denial stage—dooms rage—holy helplessness (creating its own mess) ///

Bombenhagel shelter dweller finally gone deaf enough not to give a damn if the very last shell falls and doesn't make a sound, if the blinding, white phosphorous blast burns and scars and fuses the retina to the cornea [(together)—all together now]. Unconscious, deaf and blind; might as well be dead, infact, just might be the light the blind can see, the end o' the tunnel, the pull towards, the attraction allowing *one last stop* (the same as it ever was) while observing facts of past—visions of future—patterns surrounding impressions of the Now (that just IS).

Still, some songs resonate sensually between the ears, only to ourselves, as well as between the thighs. Words re-write whole—half—quarter notes taking hold and plunging deep into our superego. Words; none of which are new, meaning they've been used, all of 'em feeling so used. What is there that is new / pictures of freedom and the serpent's script in a song / / unusual for the moment until the not so startling realization that in some other place—another fraction of time, neurons driven full force /// forces the unique madrigal sensation to blink in code, that very last refrain?? Humming a whistle and a snap and a clap on a railroad track, under the pleasantly predictable springtime sunshine (all so alone, the only original tune left in the world and its mediocre melody) cascades like heavy cream down upon the back of our collective judgment, both in time and in rhyme.

(All together now—the song we all sing)

END BALLAD

Feb. 12, 1998

(you are forced / made to / along for the ride, away we went / far away, out of the way, into the forest chilled trees and darkened treetops.)

Cab driver left you in the wrong part of town (along for the ride) it's not out of My way / I'm going past there / ya don't wanta be around this place all too long / dark man, dark. Step in, have a drink / well ya I drink and drive / I drink and walk / I drink and sit. Don't drink much do ya / well I do, don't know why / never even thought much about it / guess I just drink ta take the edge off the speed. No man, that's a joke, it's cool, ya don't have to put on your seatbelt / seatbelts are for suckers / for people who dream about what they did that previous afternoon / for people who run to stay healthy / people who balance their checkbook / people who are good spellers / never talk with their mouth full / only screw to classical music / have never pissed outside / think it's disgusting to drink from the carton / can't stand the sight of blood / know somebody who was born in Wyoming / never fried an egg / always vote / fear God / drink decaf / know when Flag Day is / never fucked in a car / enjoying planning a Vermont vacation / save birthday cards / don't know how to break a full court press / can't . . . . no, no, you can buckle-up if ya want ta, those people are neither worse nor just as good even better their not. Well, I just say things like that / don't know why / never even thought much about it / just guess it's what's bouncing around in my brain ya know??? Well, I'm gonna have another one / not for, but on the road / hold the wheel, would ya / thanks.

Feb. 13, 1998

In a race for the last glass of water on Earth, born to act out against order from chaos, uninterested hostility responds to flu-like conditions as they mutate through the callous tension of time and time / again running in place (in place of a race), as competition stands in for religion, peace of mind becomes a bedtime story heard once or twice as a child; hauntingly impatient, seemingly undeniable, life flowed [(in simple solid shapes—between the world of imaginary numbers and the moonlight of lastnight) as if by design] bypassing thought or feeling, judgment or thunder, honesty or water, in much the same manor of an overcast sunrise, or the crack inside the whip. Downside-up in the air / simulating motion; rebreather living where they all have, timetraveler's cottonwood mask samples silksurgen's precision mathematics, slinging verbal Whiskey, untiring last ditch efforts to keep sticking around a circle complete in a center called empty // full of all that was /// standing where they all have, behind yesterday's final thought, next to the potion know to have the shortest lasting side-effects centered by long division and cared for by the same west wind that brought my pen to the postpoint, lost for sure, but at least it's somewhere (else) than out in the open, "Can't have things all nice and simple now can we!?!"?!?

The Very Next Day,

[and All being still is well. (Pleasantly unpredictable) even as it was two years ago, knowing change changes, but hardly recognizing thought pattern's pattern] restless, nomadic, unsettled something still stirring stronger than the day before / after the very next day . . . . Heir / Aujourd'hui / Demain . . . .

Yesterday / Today / Tom Morrow

The man known by the name Tom Morrow lives. As a person does, does not know words created, crazy tired, cut up into zones / lines [fading out (as in pillars of smoke and ash and Yesterday and tides and questions and) the likes of which stabilize certain; sort of, kind of like, being, known as the man that lives three houses up the down street.]. / a.k.a. T.O.M.

I'd seen him Today Earl E. Er in his garden as I passed by on my way to write this. He said, "Hay, how's everything going?" In which I replied, "It's going," (shyly implying that I do not wish to stop and chat, but thank-you for your shallow concern.) I can't stand him. I dislike speaking with, or even seeing him. I'll probably see him Tomorrow.

P.S.,

As a postscript descending upon itself; being bordered by physical and personal isolation and enveloped by alien ingested, drug induced madness, this is a reminder to everybody (or more than likely just myself) that there is no perfect square (tangible) as all is real. Mathematical perfection exists only in the minds of women and men, as far as we know / knowing thoughts of visions to be perfectly plausible, reliable and undeniable infact and factor and fractions of quarter dreams; half-awake whole notes, resting on the second to last stanza of M.Y. silent symphony. 'Have A Nice Day' faces doowooping in the key of G to the domino theory's Doppler effect. First version of the harlequin's harpsichord solo, invokes a deity's daughter to resonate acappella moans somewhere between East Saint Louis and a portal to the next dimention. Appearing multigifted disspite the surrounding of auditory hallucinations, rotting away Tower of Iron Will's gatekeeper. Seemingly opposite / effect and cause casually alphabetizes daily-planner, disregards chronological chromium momentum and unknown shock value while assassin's assumptions ooze all the incorrect answers, nullifying any unasked questionless questions.

A tiny, liquid blue box (holding all words never said) rests uneasily atop the bottom of a cliff. An actual size roadmap leads to a land where sand can't be felt, felt can't be worn and wind wares away ocean sized thoughts / thought of previously, but never said, so nighttime can unfold as told [with little to do of the day (as it only gets in the way) while magic and motion renew delight] none seems all and all seems right.

HAPPY HOUR

I suddenly remember part of a dream I had last night

after I passed-out on the couch.

I was at your local tavern, quaffing ale with a room

full of strangers. I was starring directly in front of me at a sign that read

NO HAPPY HOUR ON WEEKENDS

I stood-up from my stool and in slow motion I mouthed the words,

"My name's Ed and I'm an alcoholic,"

And it felt good to admit that.

But really, I'm not.

STENCH OF THE IGUANA

-or-

BEER in the BEARD

Even now, as I sit and stare into the void at the wall in front of me, my close to sober brain can not quite fathom how I didn't notice it straight away. How callous am I to the strange spinning of everyday life? Not only did I walk unconsciously past it, but I bought it a drink after the bartender decided she had enough cash in the till at this time of day to turn my semi-hard earned paycheck into semi-hard earned, hard liquor.

"I'd like to buy the bar a round of their favorite, inexpensive beverage," I said while flashing back to grade school multiplication tables to guess my, (my drink x 9 + tip = ?), oh, I'll let the computer do it. My favorite, inexpensive, American-made malt beverage arrived with me thinking that I really should be pinching the 'ol pennies, but without remorse nor regret the mason jar, penny collection got turned into 20 class A Virginia blend, factory rolled cigarettes just this morning. So if there was to be any penny pinchin' goin' on I'd best start tomorrow. Lying in bed, along side the guilt of my late bill(s) payment(s), rests the speculative need to bring my karma closer to center and if I had to buy everybody drinks / weighed against all the free beverages I've had laid in front of me, so be it (amen).

Placing a filterless slice of bliss in smoking position I borrowed a half empty, (or half full), pack of self-promotional, bar room matches and ignited another five minutes of smoking pleasure. Hailing the leggy and obviously healthy bartender with the cigarette between my pointer and middle finger, so I can talk with my hands and feel more like Harvey Keitel in Reservoir Dogs, I gave a hitch hiking motion three barstools to my right. After she sashayed over to my position on the barley train; she placed both of her elbows on the bar, folded one arm on top of the other and starred directly at me for a full five seconds without talking, or even blinking until,

"So what (pause) it's a lizard (pause) on the bar drinking a shot of whiskey, big deal, guess what happened to me on the way to . . . ." There was nobody on either side of it and with what appeared to be about six dollars and fifty cents, 3 French fries and a business card in front of it the lizard lapped brown grain and scanned the room quietly. Its tail, which draped off the bar top, swayed with the rhythm of the blues tune trumpeting from the surround sound speakers.

"It's a chameleon," I interjected as she continued to complain of some triviality the sunrise had thrust upon her.

"Eh," she grunted, cranking her head in its direction.

"The family Chamaeleontidae, angular shaped head, independently moving eyes," I say while once again realizing that my "Discovery Channel" flash-backs creep into some odd situations.

"So," she bellowed, looking back at me.

"So," I volleyed softly in her direction then took a long drag of my smoke. A time out ensued as I exhaled, examined the sincerity in her voice and she marveled at the slight resemblance between me and every other fella she'd tried to charm a few extra tips from. "Is it yours," I asked with enough sarcasm in my voice to leave a bruise on her cheek?

"How the fuck should I know who owns it, I just fuckin' got here . . . . ," her words tapered off as she traveled down the bar to fill another mug with ale and another person's life with joy. I took my eyes off of her backside and with a sigh I focused straight ahead at the reflections of lights in the bottles of unopened hangovers. Lost for an immeasurable amount of time inside the light's hypnotic, multi-colored glow, I snapped out of my daze while I was half-way into a soft, comfortable toke of cigarette smoke. (Giving it some more thought) I cocked my head as to get a partial view of the zucchini-sized creature and exhaled with a supercilious look shaping my face; all the while wondering dryly to myself if anybody else could see it, or they do and could care less, or if it was really there, or . . . .

"Besides, you just bought it a drink. Is it yours," she cackled and zoomed down the counter to greet the next contestant on, *'Just Try And Have A Good Time'*?

And with that . . . . went my train of thought, broken like a wedding vow on a tequila sunrise. She disintegrated a chunk of perfectly good "quality time" I had to myself. That deep / not so deep meditation which originates near the same corner of the brain that gives us daydreams and mirages. Although I felt as if an operator cut my long-distance call short, this gave my bladder an opportunity to let me know that I've been ignoring its required emptying. I ventured to the commode to make room for happy hour pints of my favorite, inexpensive drink and (while I'm alone) perhaps I'll partake in a hit of the sweeter smoke, in hopes of dispelling the lizard illusion and returning to a normal intoxication session.

I floated back to my bar stool and into the cloudy chaos of a dozen, or so, patrons scrambling about the room as if they were looking for a contact lens and trying to catch a dog. I grabbed the crumpled pack of smokes off of the bar top and peered into its depths, taking a body count. As I pulled one of the last cigs standing the bartender walked by and said, "Those crazy fuckers, you should've seen 'um feed a shot of vodka to that iguana. The fuckin' thing became see-through and everybody started running around looking for it, oh man, it was funny. I got a good tip out of it though," and she shuffled down the bar to scoop up the $6.50.

I light the cigarette, took a long drag and stared at the wall in front of me.

"When asked why I prefer it silent I replied that it's much quieter than all that noise.
When asked why I replied as such, I said nothing."

—*Jimmy Keeper (on his death bed)*

The scene is as drying cement, with eleven shades gray and noon could appear at any time of day. This would be a good day to receive earth shattering news. This would be a great day to walk around and let everybody you meet know just how you feel about a day as awful and godforsaken as this one is. This is the day reserved for those who have hit the proverbial bottom, with a wet-meat slap that turns the heads of those in the immediate vicinity. This is just another day for Chaos and Confusion to team up with the icy hand of DOOM. They *knock* on the front door; let themselves in, inform the dazed resident of their intent, beat the shit out of normalcy, leave a battered, bruised and bloody victim, all the while blaming fate (or) karma (or) justice (or) the natural order of things (or) . . . .

This is one of those days where people are frequently overheard saying, "I'm having one of *those* days," and only they know what that means. This one of those days anybody would trade for an accurate and damaging blow to the back of the head. A day that reeks of theatrics, stage props, pre-recorded background noise and a tragic plot that has been reviled to all, save the main character. This is one of those days that turn happy people sad, sad people depressed, depressed people medicated, pilled people suicidal and suicidal people into statistics. A selfish bastard of a day with just enough oxygen to go around and not a molecule more.

Perhaps a comet passed too close to the Earth as the tide's of the moon pulled at their peak strength and a few major planets aligned while sunspots vomited radiation unevenly throughout the solar system. (or not). No excuses shadow today for this is a day that induces / arouses feelings that have no opposite. Feelings that come crashing down upon the most tender part of one's emotional stratosphere and suffocate the fool that were only trying to get their feet wet. So we hold our breath; swim for the surface, swim for shore, take a big gulp and get it over with. This is one of those days that will hand down it's decision ten minutes too late to do anything about it.

THE DAYS OF JIMMY KEEPER

An oozing silence coats the bedroom with an electricity of anticipation as the weight of the darkness increases ten fold, (one for each minute left before the awakening). Is all silent? All is silent. The silence from the screams afar, the silence of a falling star, a tear for fear of impending doom, the silence that envelopes the darkened room. Silence, taking on a disposition all it's own with apparent movement, growth, weight (silence weighs heavier in the nighttime air) and other propensities of an entity. Silence, dominating nothing it is not allowed to dominate, as it seems to exhibit signs of consciousness, such as its realization of its place among the events surrounding it while it in turn surrounds those very same events. More than a presence, but a force that displays frontal-lobe, decision making abilities, be it that on a subtle level. Lost somewhere in the uncharted regions of puberty, in the race for an identity amid the screaming masses, is a child unknowingly brushing up against the camouflaged power of silence. Similarly, those that have gone deaf hold on to some sort of resistance / acceptance relationship with silence that those of us with adequate hearing could never truly understand, while a similar nexus is reviled from those whom have recently died, (but shown only each to the other) never-the-less their participation in the clear murkiness is quite a bit more complex than a child's. Although death is extremely simple, it is the children that make the simplest connection with the least amount of resistance, perhaps that is due to their lack of a "mature" understanding on the concepts and actualities of the quiet nothingness, but even so, very few of the youngsters realize that their serious contact with the dimention of silence is but a game.

Remember playing, "**The silent game**"?

The first person to speak loses, starting NOW . . . .

. . . . to a seven year old child this is the ultimate test of patience and will-power considering they have so much to say in 24 hours they can't fit it all in one day. This is not to be confused with the "silent treatment" which is more of a social strategy than an adolescent game, (or something like that). The silent treatment, a weapon, has isolated, condemned and confused so many younger siblings and disobedient spouses that to this day some victims are still saying, "But, what did I do?". Silence is taught and experienced by the animals of the wild. Silence is survival, be it stalking prey, or the stillness of game. Stealth vs. Patience, a one round battle with no time limit. Fight is not an option. Hunger clouds the drive. Silence coats the participants in a fragile skin of quantum-fate where upon hangs the balance of neutrality throughout the cosmos. A temporary extenuation of life for the winner in this contest that ends only in the loser going silent.

Most of the key elements to stealth survival are taught and experienced by nearly every youth in the game adults forsake and abandon as childish. Hide-and-go-seek.

I'm going to count backwards from one-hundred and all you all better be concealed, inconspicuous and quiet otherwise I will find you, expose you and then you will be IT. (and nobody wants to be IT. IT, is not good.) This is a game where those kids who are too slow for tag get a chance to exhibit their abilities to outwit the fast, the smart and the experienced. An opportunity to gain a taste of recognition, if not respect, this sport is too good to pass up. Everybody can play, and you know what's on the line, you know the rules, let's begin.

100, 99, 98, 97 . . . . just keep betting on yourself, you're the long shot . . . . 81, 80, 79 . . . . someday you'll pay off big . . . . 68, 67, 66, 65 . . . . is it too obvious, too small to cover my, too close, too close . . . . 33, 32, 31, 30 . . . . the scramble, the evaluation, INDECISION . . . . 19, 18, 17 . . . . just chose, anything, anywhere, duck down, be quietly quiet. A choose being made at the moment the forced silence, spread thin through out the backyard, appears to be taking part in the activities. 10, 9, 8, 7 . . . . I'm too close, I'll get caught in record time . . . . 6, 5, 4 . . . . I gotta move, gotta, now, do it now . . . . 3, 2, 1 . . . . No!!! "Ready (or not), here I come!" Just you sit still now child and be quiet is the only advice to adhere to, but the silence of the playing field and the stealth of the predator quickly eats away at one's body-suit of plaster cast patience. With a heart beating so hard you might crack a rib you'd best breathe through your mouth, sit still, I know it's uncomfortable, stop shaking, here comes the counter and here IT comes. The sweat on the brow, moist palms, pressure on the bladder, sphincter tightens, stomach gurgles, you're going to explode if you don't piss your pants first.

Within the noise / silence boarder, lies a key, a different way to perceive the reality about you. It is a concept, a factor, a presence, a choice, a way of life, a way to live. Even in a sound-proof room a human will still hear two sounds. A high pitch (the nervous system) and a low pitch (the blood circulating). What does it take to experience total silence? Ask Jimmy Keeper. He has been asleep for six hours and twenty-two minutes, slipped in and out of REM sleep several times, had 16 different dreams, (only two of which he'd remember) and would normally wake in exactly ten minutes. Jimmy, now there's an individual who knows a little something about the power of silence, but it's a crying shame that seconds after his alarm clock goes off he would forget nearly all of his fantastic, prophetic visions (save the clues in his two recalled dreams). Upon awakening he would eventually realize that he has been sleeping for about six and one-half hours and remembering only those two dreams he'd divide up his sleep into 3 hour and 15 minute blocks of silence induced, sub-conscious collages. But his alarm clock doesn't spit-out its violent and rapid hammering of the metallic shells of boom until 6:52 a.m. Jimmy Keeper has ten minutes left of sleep.

With ten minutes left before the alarm induces arousal from slumber's mysterious splendor, Jimmy is presumably on another level of consciousness and unaware of the myriad of activities his body is engaged in. Unflavored, household words don't convey sleeps spellbound, dimensional-door aspect appreciated by illusionist and acid-head alike. Now, to the victim of the Sand Man one's bodily functions and life lines are not only involuntary, but do not even exist until possibly noticed by the sleeper upon awakening, or an outside observer. Nobody can imagine the reality that happens inside Jimmy's dream world, but with ten minutes left, who really cares? Mr. Jimmy Keeper, Born 11/14/62 at 7:04 p.m. in a hospital on planet Earth, contemplates death and dying as all of us have, or will, all the while half-earth tonight dreams a thanatopsis. "What would happen if I died peacefully in my sleep? Would I be aware? What if I was dreaming at my time of death? Would my death, like other outside sensations, be incorporated into my dream? Would I dream with the dead?" The fate of an awakened Jimmy Keeper is a bludgeoning of confusion provided by the significance of the organized chaos currently being acted, like a slow-motion play on the stage of excess information, under a strobe light of electrical impulses. If he was aware of how little time was remaining he might not have engineered another dream, but his biological clock is prepared to wake him (dispite his present condition and current tour of duty inside the mind's maze of doors). There is seemingly plenty of opportunity to continue dreaming. So that's just what he'll do.

*   *   *

Trapped within the hazy blur along the edge of any canyon, Jimmy Keeper steps through a door and emerges one-thousand miles away in the back of his head. Unfortunately for our hero the door happens to be on the very edge of a cliff. Through the door, on the other side, Jimmy thinks he realize that he is dreaming, but if he was aware, he would catch a subtle clue to his present position inside existence. At the exact moment Jimmy Keeper stepped through the door he experienced total silence. A moment that is reserved for living beings on rare occasions, in the natural world, or living beings at the point in time where life exits the body. And yet, there is a dream along the edge of forever that is so powerful it can stop time in its callous tracks and bring about total silence. The door is that moment in a form he can recognize and the dream is reserved for Jimmy Keeper. Balancing on the edge of timelessness by the tips of his toes, that moment fought against the forward flow of time, to brush up against his childhood and engage his brain in a type of memory fueled hide-and-go-seek.

O.K., I'm going to count backwards from ten and you all better be unaware, dizzy and silent otherwise you will be found and exposed (and no body likes to be IT). The journey from A to B with no in-between halts time in its meaningless progression, going nowhere, but coming from somewhere. Once upon a bedtime story time was the predator and Jimmy was the prey. Now, in the stillness of a moment, silence forces neutrality. Jimmy balances on the wind, grasping a door frame with the tips of his fingers until they turn as pale as the moonstruck sky. Without negotiation a deal has been signed and that exact moment is to be Jimmy's last. He will continue to exist in a timeless reality, balancing on the edge, never to fall nor ever to step back through the door.

Removed from our world, stuck in the beginning of a dream never to be had, with 5,515,579,062,000 vibrations of the microwave radiation emitted by a cesium-133 atom (during a specified atomic rearrangement) left before his alarm clock goes off, Jimmy Keeper (coated in silence) will never hear the chiming of those bells again. Suspended in mid-air over a canyon's depths, just out of reach, is a face-to-face stare down between Jimmy and his clock. The clock saying 6:42 / Jimmy saying nothing. (he preferred it silent) To the untrained eye, or outside observer this may appear to be a cruel fate, but Jimmy seems to mind the most, because his last thoughts will be heard by nothing, nobody.

As time presses on for the rest of us and today gets off to its predictable start, with alarms belching on cue, Jimmy is still wrapped in blankets and irony. His anticlimactic chant reeks of redundancy. "And if I die before I wake . . . ," echoes throughout the canyon.

GODHEAD

RECONNECT THE BURDEN PLACED UPON INFINITY

IGNORE IGNORANCE ACCEPTED AS ACCEPTABLE

DISPEL THE ILLUSION CAST UPON THE TRINITY

AND DINE IN THE FOREST ON THE WISDOM THAT IS

BOBO THE "MAGIC" DUCK

PART ONE

Expansion of the Universe

(AP) **Morgan City, LA.**—Police found the body of a 25 year-old white, male, late last night in a ditch along Railroad Avenue. The young, white male, clutching an envelope in his hand, had a letter opener thrust into his back. Homicide experts suspect MURDER . . . .

"What a vile concoction of gobble-gook," I exclaim as the slam of a daily newspaper sends a shockwave of bottles crashing to the floor from yawn-dizzying heights! "Who do they think there're tryin' to fool? (everybody) Humans die everyday in every way. Who decides which particular portion of violence is attractive enough to arouse interest in the general public? Is it our 'Constitutional Right' to read brief overviews of stories of slanted truths printed by bureaucratically bogus, big business news papers?" (short pause as I realize that I'm speaking to myself)

Although a nowhere subject this was an adequate topic to discuss with myself, in my less than pleasant mood, as I made a bold attempt to remove debris from the rummage-sale coffee table, which curiously enough contained no coffee (save the traces in the ring stains). I find this lack of coffee slightly disturbing considering the massive amount in which I consume on an 'average' day. Coffee, bong-hits and pastries, a morning greeting ceremony capable of giving me an advantage on even the worst of days (such as ones that begin without coffee and start with a daily newspaper?). Then again, for me and me alone, this was not to be an 'average' day. I had that, "something abnormal has been set in motion," feeling and should have acted on it somehow; as I carried twelve cheep, empty, domestic beers and today's local news, into the kitchen and dispose of them in the trash bag that rested uncomfortably in a cardboard box.

Ignoring my intuition and focusing on my stomach I move to shed light into the ever-chilly darkness of the refrigerator and again I find my complex psyche disturbed at the vision before me. Noticeably distraught, I was callous to the physical hunger as I started to drool and moan at the pure vastness of the extra tall, extra empty fridge. It appeared so much larger and whiter and brighter than I remember it being, so much so that I got to wondering if this was the very same fridge that I've been storing booze and condiments in for the last four months. A quick, useless check in the vegetable crisper could be described as predictable, but instead of accounting for my every action I just lay a blank stare inside in hopes that the rumbling of my stomach might call forth some ancient, mystical, anti-hunger spell, but alas, the response falls nothing short of predictable.

Thinking that I knew what would cure those mid-morning, nothing to do, hangover blues I returned to the "living room" and the stolen, one cushion missing couch and scanned the area for paraphernalia. I swear I knew for sure that my pipe was on the floor next to the corner of the faded lime-green, manufacturing mistake of a couch, but that particular section of the universe had become so engrossed by an encampment of dust bunnies that I dared not venture in. This instantly became of minor importance once I glanced at an empty, crumpled, plastic bag on the milk-crate endtable, signaling the completion of a cycle *and the dawn of a quest.*

I can admit, if only to myself, that I was down and fading fast. The day had the jump on me, but I could not, I would not give-up, I would not be denied. The quest must move on (forward). I swear that I know for sure that there is something, just out of sight, that is willing to be scraped clean of its magical resins. Thus begins the chant. "Here pipe, pipe, pipe, pipe. Pipe, pipe, here pipe," repeats between my ears as I embark on a thorough search of the overpriced, underkept, apartment from corner to dusty corner. I even make a half-assed spelunker of the twenty-two year old, poky-springy, kind of musty smelling couch and come up with nothing except a coupon for 55 cents off any HORMEL product and an old, broken unbreakable comb, (both of which I placed back into their sepeltura).

(The following is a portion of the inner-monologue used to get my mind off the word "pipe" as I search: "Between dirty underwear and the Serenity

Prayer I search my search the 'high' search. A natural observer, or trained onlooker, I'm great, no, wonderful at finding things of great, yeah, great importance. I'd smoke toenails if it had the same effect. Sailing a sea of plastic and man-made, natural grain wood, disguised as a picture inside of a puzzle of an underfurnished, overpriced vessel, taunting and concealing some variation of the mighty hemp plant. Treading water in an ocean of urban renewal where man, commander of plastic, blind and drunk, directs the vessel and I, as a peasant crew member of this rented life, scrape the deck for my controlling interest in the conglomerate [the organization]. [nothing] One who dares to brave the sea of mediocrity [nothing] in order to better one's self, relatively thinking, or the world around, also relative, [nothing] would hope, no, expect to [nothing] find much more booty than I, as Captain Jones, [nothing] have.")

I was amazed, to put it simply, at how sharp of an angle my bad to worse day takes just by opening the front door.

With hands on hips, a sigh is heaved and a statement is made. "There's not much left for me here," I declare as I change out of my dirty shirt and into a slightly less dirty shirt. An anticlimactic exit was only appropriate, so out the apartment door I went. I instinctively keep the door unlocked, (the lord of the land has yet to present me with a key to my own place of living, as was promised somewhere around the time the toilet and thermostat were to be "checked into"). Such is life in the city and I deal with it through adaptation, I have nothing, worth the risk of being caught, to take.

As I reach for the handrail, out of the corner of my left eye (or my good eye) I spot the stair light (or hall light) as being illuminated and suspiciously freeze my forward motion. With a slow motion, half-step, back-step and a pivot I peer into the filthy covering. At first with my, "What you say 'bout my mama," look I wondered how long it had been since anybody cleaned this dusty, bug graveyard, light cover. Then I remembered how filthy, oily and dirty I felt and proceeded to say what I was originally thinking, "How long have you been on?"

The light bulb, with its, "I've been on fifteen days, you've just been too stoned to notice," look, didn't speak a word. Not that I expected a response, but one wouldn't have shocked me. What would have shocked me is if the light bulb spoke English, fuckin' thing's made in Bora Bora and I'm not even sure where that is, much less what language they speak. Feeling deflated and defeated somehow, I reach into the apartment and pull the light switch down. On my second attempt to descend the staircase I declined the use of the safety hand rail, because if my safety depended on the quality of that railing, I'd rather risk the journey without. Stair by stair, recalling through negative reinforcement to duck in the appropriate spot, or rather a bump on the skull, I come closer to my confrontation with the physical barrier by taking a firm, upright stance. And then, the door.

> "The door the door without a care
> Beyond the door you best beware
> The outside world gets inside your head
> !the door! Turn around go back to bed"

—Public restroom author unknown

Unsure of where my walk will take me, I realize once again why I hesitate to turn the knob. The general public, with its meaningless small talk and disapproving, judgmental stare, only begins my list of cultural anxieties that seems to grow steadily larger through out the years. Disgust, not shame, is the driving force behind my five or six day hold-ups inside the apartment. It's not a hermits life in the city, though the large number of humans and creatures attempts to mask an individual. Nearly every morning I tend to find the not-so-general public asleep on my couch, or floor, or under the kitchen table, or a roommates bed, or scattered about my own, personal sleeping quarters. Perhaps waking and finding nobody about the apartment added to the strange air that I've been inhaling. Perhaps the sunny and relatively pleasant afternoon that awaited my arrival knew that all I could think of was how "god damn bright" it was going to be on my bad eye as well as my good eye. The squeaking sound of the opening of the door sets off a sub-conscious signal and my mechanical walk and cold stare are prepared to engage, but at the end of one full rotation of the front door knob, a not too mysterious figure went through the motions of opening the door to come in and jumped back at the unexpected sight of somebody opening the door to go out.

Luke, Luke G., Luke G. Honkey Commando, Luke has weed, Luke always has weed, Luke makes sure that he has pot on his person at all times, (it's the law of the bag pincher).

"You're not going OUTSIDE are you," Luke jests.

"Got any weed Luke," I say ignoring his opening comment?

"N-N-No. (pause) D-Do you," Luke says with nervous laughter? "Where ya off ta," he asks changing the subject?

"Nowhere, I'm just off."

I know he has some, Fuckin' A, this rattles my cage. When we first met I kept him high for weeks at a time and now, now this petty, pinchie, pinching, pincher has taken complete control of my day.

"Tryin' to scrape up change for coffee," I added.

"How much you need," politely asking?

"All of it," I reply in disgust.

It was only a split second before his hand was in and out of his front, right pocket exposing a hand full of change, reaffirming my belief that he has some marijuana even deeper in that pocket. Plucking three quarters from his tight grip, Luke offers them in good will, (I'm sure).

"Wow, thanks 'G'," I say with a glimmer of hope for the day. This is followed by a long moment of awkward silence while I place the currency in my pocket and Luke scrambles to think of an excuse to walk off of the front steps and around the corner before he gets pinned into revealing the 4 grams of Mexican brick weed cowering in his left sock.

The silence dragged on, weighing heavy upon the back of Luke's neck, smothering him to the point of moist palms and butterflies in his stomach.

"Well, (pause) I'm gonna cruise, (long pause) check ya latter," Luke said and jumped off the steps, cut through the back yard towards some downtown bench where he can pick and choose who he wants to catch a buzz, the whole while complimenting himself on how he slinked his way out of another undesirable situation.

I didn't even hear him say the word "cruise" as I was preoccupied with the unusually large amount of mail in my mailbox. I was actually startled when I looked up and Luke wasn't anywhere to be seen. I took it as a good thing and started on my way towards the local family restaurant, with a fist full of mail, to search for the bottom of the bottomless cup of coffee.

$537.27—electricity bill, to (former) resident, Mr. Tryda Findus.
$99.12—record/tape/CD club bill, sent to (former) resident, Mr. Richard Cranium.
$120.50—cable bill, sent to (former) resident, Richard Cranium.
An advertisement, sent to current resident, from the Big Giant SavemoreMart Company Inc. (thinking the general public recognizes paper on the street as garbage, I instantly toss the "Bargain of the Year Sale Spectacular" out onto the road and skimmed the rest of the mail.)

Final notice, Richard Cranium.
Final notice, Tryda Findus.
Final, Final Notice, Richard Cranium.
Vote "Maybe" on referendum 17, Tuesday the 12th, resident.
Final notice, Richard Cranium.
Re-elect Mayor James (something or other) on the 26th. Our slogan, "You've had worse Mayors, admit it." (I sigh as truth in advertising and politics collide head on, forming a bloody, flaming pool of despair.)
$1,212.12 Past due, post final notice credit card bill, sent to former resident, Bob Smith.

"What's this," I wonder out loud as I spot the County's address stickers adorning it?

"City of blah, county of blah, vs. blah, in accordance to county codes and such (per say) National Standards in violation of city ordinance *2947.18* chapter *9*, paragraph *14*, section *2*, where as by defendant in question did here by, unlawfully, without regard to other parties involved in said incident, on said date, violated such code(s) as previously stated and shall give up a sum of no less than *$1100.50*, loss of driving privileges for not less than *5* years, serve *200* hours of community service, make *3* letters of apology, of not less than *400* words (each), to said parties involved."

I felt guilty, embarrassed and a tad bit nervous, but wasn't positive of what heinous crime I've been found guilty of. Although if I thought hard I'm sure I'd recall, but as it stands, the entire stack of wasted paper, ink and postage becomes the first resident of the nearest garbage bin which oddly enough sparks an out of context, karmic thought circle. For two, mind boggling minutes, I had to wonder what the hell Luke came over for. I am now so sure my day can not get any worse that I disregard the County Circuit Court letter and the whole of my morning and proceed to enter the local family restaurant.

*   *   *

(Am I to be forever trapped within my inability to express, a lack of something or other, defying natural growth and expansion, (inward) collapsing upon itself (eventually) and denying the potential? A dream in a nightmare making a memory that never happened and turning it into a truth never told, denying its potential. Am I here in this place thinking these thoughts that none may never know? Hanging on a point in time known as a moment, we assume a dominant position over our mental and emotional status. Emotions blend and build to the flashpoint; a line of no definition, crossing all boundaries, untouched by ego, untarnished by good. I suffocate under the crush of impending doom that is never to expose truth. Chaos wears no mask, takes all of the blame and even cleans up after itself (sometimes). My mask, molded by that very potential I deny, is on display, hanging on a nail in the exact center of the flashpoint. From beyond the shadows, as if it were never hiding, came a moment. Is it thee moment, the BIG one, the last straw, the lighting of the fuse? One can never tell. One will never know. Until.

The most specific and consistent reply obtained by local police, from eye witnesses at the scene was that, "A young man was drinking coffee and for some unknown reason went crazy," although stories ranged from; "(He) was doing drugs in the bathroom and right there on the table, I saw him and then (he) started screaming and throwing things," to, "There were two of them, they both looked Iranian or something, one (of them) threw a fit and the other guy vanished, it was probably all a distraction, check the register, CHECK THE REGISTER."

Officially an unidentified male, caucasian, age 18-25, entered a local family restaurant, ordered a $0.79 cup of caffeinated coffee and upon receiving the bill started to act out random acts of violence, then departed the establishment after placing $0.75 on the cash register. The register was opened to make an accurate count of all funds and the remaining coffee was rushed to the lab for analysis.

PART TWO

Collapsing of the Universe

To ask for forgiveness, (personal satisfactory salvation), to justify one's self reasoning for acts motivated by instinct, to ponder the damning question "WHY", all a waste of energy. An energy that is limited by body. When energy is limited by form it lacks quantum movement, or the potential to invoke 'free movement' upon itself. Full force is suppressed in exchange for time. Time for reaction and adjustment to changes. Simply noting the importance of the fundamental physical fact that the arrow of time always points forward causes ones relative history to become history, history class to become a rather silly concept and "You can't go back", the motto of human decision making. Energy of self increases when memories are made, new ground is covered and thoughts flow undisturbed, (forward).

"There's not much left for me here," I declare as I look back at the town that once held me and currently holds many others, whether they know it or not, behind its economic prison bars. People waste their energy in today's contradictory society and the distractions that embody everyday existence. I'm gone, I'm out of there, I'm (as they say) history. It didn't matter what geographic direction I moved in, although I'm sure it was west, as long as I kept moving, free flowing, away, (forward). Off the off road, closer to nature and further from culture, where the true winds blow and the wild cannabis does grow. The hunger, directed by my stomach, would now be satisfied with a teaspoon of natures ingrown inspiration. Off the highway, off the black top, off the road of gravel, off the path of dirt I blaze a trail through the forest. Looking for nothing, I find my everything. Noticing the absence of mechanical sounds invading my ears and raping my brain I meld into the essence of life, (life's own energy). The fox does not fear the spider, they have nothing to exchange, but the absence of one effects the presence of the other. The massive oak tree does not hoard sunlight for its personal use on cloudy days, it is that very light that is responsible for it size. The other trees under the oak grow to their fullest potential; be it large, small, or in between. (When its dark, nothing receives the light.) For now, one of the in between trees currently shades my sore feet, as well as the rest of my body. The sounds of the forest soothes me as does a symphony, each sound taking its turn, then for a few exquisite measures they play in unison, then again break into solos, duets, trios. I almost lost myself, my thoughts, my memories past and future, inside the sounds of the forest floor. Almost.

"Quack, quack, (pause) quack, quack," rudely interrupted mother natures fantasy in D minor. At first I was unsure that I was hearing what my brain registered me as hearing, especially during an all orchestral, four measure pause, but as it repeated over and over I focused on the monotone sound and the actuality of it sounding like a child, on helium, saying the word, "quack."

"A duck (pause) in the woods," I say out loud hoping a duck would waddle from under the brush and relieve my now overpowering, curiosity. As the next set of "quacks," started I stood up to feel the throbbing miles upon my feet. I just had to see this duck; this poor, lost, dumb creature. The lakes a dozen miles away, what was it doing here? I covered my eyes and face with my right hand and forearm and blazed a new trail, one through the thick underbrush. The sound of stick breaking from blind path making did nothing to muffle the quacking that became gradually louder and faster the closer I got to it, until there was a white noise meshing of cracking and quacking. I had picked up so much speed that I was high kneeing it up a slight incline and tripped over nothing as the hill dropped off and there were no branches, no trees, just grass and (well, what do you know) a small pond, in which momentum introduced me to. Landing on my ass after a forward somersault and up to my navel in water, I spot a duck.

It was a yellow duck, (no shit) that looked like Ernie's rubber ducky except twice as large and child-like in appearance. It made no movement save a slight bobbing motion. As I pulled myself from the pond and sat on dry ground I noticed the duck didn't even quack, it just floated there. I burst into laughter, softly at first, but soon enough I was in the mists of a powerful laughter that had me rolling over and clutching my stomach. I wasn't certain why I was laughing, because I was having too much fun doing it, but I was certain that the duck was laughing right along with me. "Oh my, I'm losing it," I thought with tears in my eyes. "What's so funny," I asked sarcastically, getting my laughter down to a chuckle? When it didn't respond I broke out into a second fit of laughter that rivaled the first. This was short lived though, as the air in my lungs had better places to be and my lips became glued together. Stunned and confused with a shot of curiosity I focused on its bill, which seemed to magnify ten times as I waited for the slightest movement. "What did you say," squeezed between my lips as I was positive the duck spoke during my laughter? The nine second pause was as 9 hours. It was the longest pause I've ever experienced, I was unaware that nine seconds could last so long. At the opening of the next second the duck responded.

"I was asking *you*, 'what's so funny?'"

I intended on saying that I think it's my lack of daily marijuana intake, or my over indulgence on LSD years ago, or perhaps I figure-out why Luke came over this morning and it struck me as hilarious, but somehow, "I don't know," tumbled out like the fifth amendment of conversations.

"I guess while you stare wide eyed and slack jawed at something as simple as a duck, I'll take this time to change your life, or at least I have the potential to do so," the duck said, sounding less like Donald Duck than one might think. "Call me BOBO."

I reacted by closing my mouth, blinking a few times and checking for signs of a hallucinatory flashback to explain this scenario. "I'm not just an ordinary, talking, yellow duck," it stated, "I'm a magical duck, I can do wonderful things." The duck paused, but as the silence became noticeably long I unconsciously blurted out, "Like what, what can you do," as I felt I really had to know? Upon completing that sentence I realized its rude tone and the fact that I just had my first dialogue with a duck and I closed my mouth, retracted my lips and bit down on them, as to not let words pop out so easily again. With the strong, solid stare of a sharp shooter I queasily anticipate, divine confirmation, but wouldn't be startled if everything vanished into a hazy blackness and I awoke in my apartment.

"I can do wonderful things; I can relieve the burdens of your everyday existence, I can take away, forever, your need for money, clothing, housing, vehicles . . . ," on and on the duck listed all of the doodads, gadgets, gimmicks, gizmos, things and watchamacallits it could take care of, all to alleviate my stress. It truly sounded wonderful. " . . . social security numbers, telephone numbers, zip codes, police . . . ," every word invoking an image that lowered my guard, toned down my defense, took a chunk from my defensive wall. At the end of its speech the duck paused with dramatic intent, then spoke. " . . . and all you have to do is speak the magic words, 'I WANT TO BE LIKE YOU.'"

It didn't speak again, it hovered on the surface skin of the water as if it had never spoke at all. I, on the other hand, was so unsettled that when the duck reviled to me the "magic" words, it was a buzz-kill. Those didn't sound like magic words, especially coming from a rubber ducky. Then again, I've never encountered a yellow, rubber ducky, in the wild, that wasn't magical. This being my first, I couldn't jump to conclusions. The intensity of the electricity generated from my brain contemplating made my vision blurry, I got light headed, I felt punch drunk, slap happy, I didn't even notice myself repeating that most mystic of incantations, "I WANT TO BE LIKE YOU."

I sat, floating in the water for a few moments, stunned as I watched a small girl jump for, what apparently was, joy. The forest swallowed her up as she giggled and danced her way through the present and into the future. The confusion I felt was soothing compared to the feeling that fired through my feathered body upon seeing my reflection in the pond. I didn't want to be a duck. I must admit that I was not lied to, I was no longer dependent upon the social necessities that caused me (and many others) much grief. I honestly contemplated, if only for a precious moment, what life as a duck would be like. Honestly. Relative perception became an expansion of consciousness. Words took on new meanings. Being a duck I'm free from human rhetoric; the number game, the head games, pointless, unfair, one-sided human games. The games people play. Then. Words. Words such as water pollution, deforestation and duck season came into focus on a pure, survival wavelength and reminded me that no matter what the positive side is, I did not want to be a duck.

EPILOGUE

The Big Bang Revisited

Day to night, night to day and back again and again became one, one became the other, becomes the other. They were never separate, they flow as one as always, together (forward). Time is almost meaningless to a duck, although it remains in a constant forward motion it is without definition. Hours, weeks, weekends, seconds, unknown, never happened. I didn't know how long I was a duck, but I believe that I had lived a duck's life to its fullest potential, aside from mating season, and I greatly desired to be human again. It was that desire, that powerful longing to "be" that molded my masks potential to fit the moment. Inside the flashpoint, at the expense of an unsuspecting nature lover, I made the moment. I made the moment be.

"Hello," I said to the stunned hiker, "My name is Beau, you can call me BOBO. I'm no ordinary, talking, yellow duck, (pause for effect). I can do wonderful things."

BVG